GOING FOR GROWTH

GOING FOR GROWTH

Realizing the Value of Technology

JOHN V. BUCKLEY

PA Consulting Group

McGraw-Hill
New York   San Francisco   Washington, D.C.   Auckland   Bogotá
Caracas   Lisbon   London   Madrid   Mexico City   Milan
Montreal   New Delhi   San Juan   Singapore
Sydney   Tokyo   Toronto

Library of Congress Cataloging-in-Publication Data

Buckley, John V.
    Going for growth : realizing the value of technology / John
V. Buckley.
       p.   cm.
    ISBN 0-07-008781-4
    1. Research, Industrial—Economic aspects. 2. Technological
innovations—Economic aspects. I. Title.
    HC79.R4B83   1998
    658.5—dc21   97-37292
                                                     CIP

*HC
79
.R4
B83
1998*

McGraw-Hill

*A Division of The **McGraw-Hill** Companies*

1 2 3 4 5 6 7 8 9 0 DOC/DOC 9 0 2 1 0 9 8 7

ISBN 0-07-008781-4

*The sponsoring editor for this book was Susan Barry, the editing
supervisor was Caroline R. Levine, and the production supervisor was
Pamela Pelton. It was set in Fairfield by Priscilla Beer of McGraw-Hill's
Professional Book Group composition unit.*

Printed and bound by R. R. Donnelley & Sons Company.

McGraw-Hill books are available at special quantity discounts to use
as premiums and sales promotions, or for use in corporate training
programs. For more information, please write to the Director of
Special Sales, McGraw-Hill, 11 West 19th Street, New York, NY
10011. Or contact your local bookstore.

This book is printed on recycled, acid-free paper
containing a minimum of 50% recycled, de-inked fiber.

To family, friends, and colleagues. And especially in memory of Dad.

CONTENTS

CHAPTER SEVEN. MANAGING CREATIVITY TO DELIVER TECHNOLOGY LEADERSHIP 107

FOREWORD

In *Through the Looking Glass*, Alice and the Red Queen had to run fast just to stay in the same place. A modern chief executive's life is much the same. With all the events and pressures that occur on a daily basis, it is always difficult to keep the company going—just at the same level of performance.

But even this of course is not enough. The company and its products cannot rest on their laurels. There is always the need to improve and refine the current set of products, because the competition is always doing the same. And, every few years, there is the imperative to come up with the next-generation product that, if successful, will trounce existing competition and ensure a successful life for the company.

It is this last imperative which, coming on top of everything else, is often the most challenging to the chief executive. How can successful new product introduction be accomplished? What systems and processes need to be put in place to ensure that this task will be successfully accomplished within a time-frame that beats the competition to the marketplace? Interestingly, firms respond differently to this challenge, emphasizing one or another activity within the firm, and allocating resources quite differently from one firm to another.

Nowhere can this be seen more starkly than in the R&D function. Firms adopt entirely dissimilar approaches to the amount of resources they put into the first part—research—or the second part—development. For both the R and the D, firms adopt different approaches to whether the various activities are kept in-house or are outsourced. The amount of expenditure in these areas varies dramatically, as a percentage of revenues or profits, from one competitor to the next. Above all, few firms operate a clear financial and business model that allows them to take rational R&D decisions, based upon the fundamental principle of what a particular decision will do in terms of value created or destroyed for the shareholders of that firm.

None of this should be surprising. The majority of chief executives will see R&D as an investment, and will know that the key to shareholder value creation is the potential return on that investment. Nonetheless putting in a model that will appropriately calculate the ROI for a given decision—indeed having a model which correctly identifies, up ahead, all the decisions that need to be taken—is problematic given the extraordinary complexity of the task at hand. Moreover, many firms appropriately see the R&D decision not as an option, but as a survival issue. A pharmaceutical company must turn out a regular procession of successful new drugs over the years. A car maker must introduce a successful model that will leapfrog the competitors at regular intervals. A software maker has to upgrade the product annually or even sooner to keep ahead of the competition. For every firm, the need to innovate and refine is constant. Seeing the matter as a survival issue can often obscure the need for a disciplined and systematic approach to each decision.

In this book, John Buckley comes up with a model that makes sense of this complex decision arena, and allows the chief executive to make those decisions which are needed to keep the firm growing and developing ahead of its competitors. Moreover, he offers a series of insights which will seem counterintuitive to many chief executives as they grapple with the problem of R&D. He offers six fundamental principles for realizing the value of technology:

1. Innovation is essential for survival.
2. Selecting the technology winners is crucial—and there are proven methods to accomplish this.
3. Technology leadership derives from well-managed creativity.
4. R&D must be accountable and managed to deliver on time and within budget.
5. There is a distinction between "Research" and "Development" which can and must be exploited.

6. Returns can only be maximised if the business and technology strategies are fully integrated.

As we enter the next millennium the most successful firms will be those that embrace "innovation" to create competition-beating products. PA Consulting Group has repeatedly demonstrated that the organization which engages in product innovation as opposed to simple product development, will become a market leader and, in the process, dramatically enhance its shareholder value.

Some argue that the future of all technology-based firms lies in the hands of their technologists. John argues that rather, the only person in the firm who can truly unlock and manage the company's full potential is the chief executive.

The first step in accomplishing this is for the chief executive to insist on greater integration (or "fusion") between the business strategy and the technology strategy of the firm. It is imperative that if the chief executive and his or her senior managers have decided on a particular strategic direction, the technologists must be working on projects which support that strategy.

Second, the chief executive must oversee the rigorous execution of this fused strategy—a phase which requires very close working between marketing, production, and R&D. R&D must have a portfolio that covers the whole spectrum, from projects producing short-term benefits to longer term breakout projects with major promise, all clearly linked to the overall business strategy.

Third, the chief executive must constantly ensure that the whole R&D process is delivering measurable value for the business. In trying to value R&D projects, it is impossible to completely eliminate the uncertainty of the future, but this need not be a reason for failing to put in place a process to support informed decision-making.

To achieve its potential and provide the level of return to shareholders that is increasingly demanded of firms, the role of R&D in firms has to change. More enlightened firms are abandoning "blue sky" research because it does not contribute to revenue and has no tangible financial output. But the most radical change has yet to take place—the management of the R&D function as a commercial asset, fully integrated with the overall business strategy.

R&D can and should be evaluated in the same way as other business investments. PA has developed a portfolio of tools, reviewed by John Buckley in this book, which have enabled our clients to revive the innovation process. Such clients—leading organizations around the world—are now reaping the benefits and leapfrogging their competitors.

This book argues, and as a chief executive myself I fully endorse, that it is the chief executive's responsibility to manage R&D to deliver the necessary return on investment that will both satisfy the shareholders and fuel profitable growth. This does not mean that the chief executive will need to become a technologist. But it does mean ensuring that the technologists are managed as any other part of the company.

What of the future? John shows that even now, technologies proliferate, products become multitechnology based, customers become more demanding, and the pressure for faster return on investment grows. As a result, ever fewer firms are likely to survive on their own R&D resources. The response is likely to be a growing trend toward outsourcing, the advent of the "virtual" R&D organization, and the setting up of collaborative agreements between firms. The choice of a particular sourcing option will depend on the culture of the firm, the confidence of the R&D organization, its propensity to accept change, the priorities of senior management, and the nature of the technologies that the firm needs to develop.

As an organization specializing in technology consulting, PA has shown that well-planned and managed outsourcing options will provide more entrepreneurial firms with a wider technology base to support national and international growth. PA believes that the technology leaders of the future will be those organizations which manage the balance of in-house and outsourced resources in a structured and timely way.

In many organizations, the R&D function is perceived—

and sometimes perceives itself—as playing by a different set of rules from the rest of the business. The problem is often compounded because R&D may be structurally isolated from the rest of the organization. Yet if senior management is to deliver growth from technology, it has to get to grips with the whole question of R&D's relationship with the rest of the firm. Culture is one aspect of this, organizational status is the other.

The foundation for future success must be the metamorphosis of the R&D function into one that fully supports the company's growth and dramatically increases shareholder value. John Buckley's book shows that now, more than ever, the chief executive must take the ultimate responsibility for managing R&D, to take their firm into the next century as a market leader.

Jon Moynihan
Group Chief Executive
PA Consulting Group

ACKNOWLEDGMENTS

I am not a technologist. My career started as a technician in what was then the old British Post Office [now known as British Telecom (BT)] where over a period of many years I became a telecommunications networking specialist. I have spent over 10 years at PA within the Computers and Telecommunications Group, working with clients to develop and apply their information technology (IT) systems. A spell as Head of PA's Business Transformation Group got me involved in helping clients apply mainstream business activities such as business process reengineering, performance improvement, TQM, and human resource development—traditional services in which PA gained its initial reputation.

In 1994 Jon Moynihan asked me to take over the management of the Global Technology Group. Almost uniquely among the major consulting firms, this part of PA's business actually produces real hardware and software products for clients, such as innovative drug delivery devices, machines for analyzing taints in meat, mobile telephone handsets, a tonometer for testing for glaucoma, an auto vending french fries machine, and many others.

My initial reaction on taking up this new assignment was one of excitement and, indeed, the experience of working with my colleagues has been exciting and enjoyable. However, the realization soon hit me that most of PA's people in my new group would be scientists and engineers—experts in technology and used to working in R&D and product development environments. I did not have that background. Could I be effective without it?

As part of a regular strategic review of our business, but also to help answer this question, my new colleagues and I undertook an analysis of the services provided for our clients and, importantly, of the role that technology should be playing in the development of our clients' businesses. It soon became clear to us that an unnecessary mystique often surrounded the technologists and the R&D groups within many of our client organizations. We came to the conclusion that PA as a whole could play an important part in breaking down the technology barriers and in helping clients leverage the technology skills in their firms, to grow revenues and profits. To develop my knowledge of technology I read many books and many articles. However, I noticed that most books on the subject had a tendency to go into the detail of the technologies and technology issues and none gave senior managers (or professional advisers like me) insights into the business issues relating to technology. We therefore decided to produce our own book on the subject. This is the result. I am indebted to my colleagues throughout PA, and the many clients I have met—particularly those included in the case studies—for contributing to my knowledge of the subject.

It would have been impossible for me to have produced this book without calling on the knowledge, experience, and deep skills of many PA consultants throughout the world. Here I acknowledge their excellent work. I hope I have managed to do justice to their expertise.

Chapter 1 summarizes the key points of the book. Chapter 2 then explains the different stages of research and development, based on input from Martin Wooler and Ann Baker, both of whom are experts in technology consulting.

Chapter 3 covers how firms should be maximizing returns from business and technology strategies. The model in this chapter has its genesis in a model produced by Jon Moynihan, Chief Executive of PA, based on his series of papers on the subject of shareholder value. The references to business simulation modeling owe a lot to the excellent work done by Ken Cooper and his team at Pugh Roberts Associates (part of PA Consulting Group) in Boston, Massachusetts. Other valuable inputs on option modeling processes were provided by Stephen Black in Cambridge and John Andersen in PA's Projects Group in London.

Chapter 4 addresses the issues of picking technology winners. This draws on groundbreaking work on defining customer needs in new product developments, using the customer value analysis (CVA) process developed by colleagues such as David Cook and Peter Fisk in London. Further valuable input based on CVA assignments was provided by John Edwards of PA's Asia Pacific Group. The technology radar process and concept discussed in this chapter were originally developed by my colleague Brian Condon.

Chapter 5 covers the innovation processes and exploits the knowledge and experience of the Technology Consulting Practice in Cambridge and in particular the insights of my fellow PA consultants Paul Barrett and Roger Scott.

Chapter 6 on managing the delivery process called on the excellent research from the outsourcing survey done by John Little and Hugh Josty in the Computers and Telecommunications Group of PA. Steven Harris's insights into the application of core competencies in analyzing and integrating acquisitions were also of great value, as was Andrew Blaxland's and Simon Tarsh's expertise in mergers and acquisition projects.

Chapter 7 focuses on managing creativity and draws on the expertise of Bridget Skelton and Jonathon Hogg in PA's HR Consulting Practice. Valuable input was also provided by Steven Bowns in PA's Cambridge Technology Centre.

In addition to the above, valuable encouragement and contributions were made by many other PA colleagues including Gavin Barrett from PA's Sundridge Park Management Centre, Mike Bissett in Technology Consulting, Bernard Eccles (Head of U.S. Consulting), Alec MacAndrew (Head of PA's Product and Process Engineering Practice), and Ali Pourtaheri (Head of PA's Communications and Electronic Systems Practice). Jenny Montier has encouraged and pushed me to get to the end of the road and she, together with Howard Firth, helped shape the case studies. Angela Plumb, my personal assistant, has done a sterling job of turning out and keeping track of the various drafts. I am indebted to her for not saying "oh no not another change!"

Two other people were major contributors to this book: John Marriage, with his overall knowledge of R&D processes, provided me with a lot of base information and thoughts drawing on his many years of industrial and consulting experience in R&D. Johanna Quintrell helped significantly in the original shaping of the structure of the book and pushed, guided, and encouraged the process of keeping the messages simple and succinct. I am indebted to them both.

Finally, the first draft was produced on what was meant to be a holiday in Mauritius. Without the encouragement and tolerance at this time of my wife Judy and her forbearance throughout, this project would never have gotten off the ground. Thank you.

John V. Buckley

INTRODUCTION

Most industrial and service organizations have now been through the discipline of improving business performance through cost reduction programs or, in the vernacular of the late eighties and early nineties, have reengineered their business processes. The results of these process improvements or reengineering exercises have varied, to say the least. Some organizations swear that the investment—sometimes several tens of millions of dollars—has proved to be of significant benefit and return. Others are lamenting, as they did over some of the total quality management projects of the eighties, that it has not been a particularly useful expenditure of either money or resources.

In the United States, most large organizations, whether successfully or unsuccessfully applying these new business processes, have achieved at least some streamlining of the business. In most instances, this streamlining has resulted in a downsizing of staff and a consequential reduction in costs. In many cases, the organizations now recognize that they have probably taken out as much cost as they want, or are able, to do. Having recognized that cost reduction and quality improvements have been done to death, many organizations are now realizing that the route to success (measured by improvements in shareholder value) is to increase the volume of the business and to increase it profitably. This is now termed *going for growth.*

The question is how this "going for growth" should be managed. Obviously, the marketing and sales departments will come under pressure to increase market share, increase sales, increase prices, and so on, to show improvements in the bottom line. However, the firm will need to show increases in top-line revenue by increasing volume, on the basis that costs within the company are now under control and can continue to be controlled as it grows.

There is one part of the organization that nearly always has huge potential for increasing volume and profitability but, often, no one seems very concerned whether it delivers real value to the organization or not. It is frequently referred to as the R&D department. For many years, the R&D department has had a mystique associated with it. It is recognized as being scientifically oriented and engineering-based, often "divorced" from the rest of the organization, having very little to do with the marketing and sales departments and, very frequently, not focused on the requirements of the firm, let alone on its customers. For years, debates have raged about the role R&D should play in support of business objectives.

The role of the R&D department is to translate the needs of the market and of the organization's customers into competition-beating products—at the right cost, the right quality, and the right level of technological sophistication—that will have the maximum positive impact on the organization's profits. The people in R&D should not be regarded as non-revenue-generating—or even more demeaning, as a cost overhead, and treated as such by the rest of the business. Increasingly, every member of the R&D organization, when he or she arrives for work each morning, should be absolutely clear that the work he or she does that day has a major part to play in the current and future success of the company.

For this to happen, a fundamental change must take place at the most senior level, that is, at the level of the chief executive and his or her management team. They have to recognize that going for growth and, hence, increasing shareholder value through R&D is a management and not a technological or scientific issue, which they must address and manage. The chief executive and the senior management team therefore need to understand what should be happening within the R&D department and how they can apply pressure at the various points of the value chain within the organization to ensure that R&D, manufacturing, operations, marketing, and sales are working together to provide the products that their customers want today and are going to be happy to buy tomorrow.

UNDERSTANDING THE DISTINCTION BETWEEN "RESEARCH" AND "DEVELOPMENT"

Most senior managers do not have a scientific or engineering background. If they do, they have probably forgotten more about science or engineering than they can remember. Over the last 10 or so years, their focus has tended to be on finance, marketing, and the broader business issues that they have to deal with on a day-to-day basis. As a result, most senior managers, whether they admit it or not, can be very intimidated by the technologists who report to them, simply because the technology of the firm is something that they will not be used to dealing with on a daily basis.

The term R&D, in itself, is enough to intimidate, or turn off, even the most aggressive and hard-nosed business manager, including the chief executive. The reason is that no one likes to be seen to be less than conversant on the topic being discussed. The problem with most technologists is that no matter how much they are encouraged to keep to a high level of abstraction in their discussions with other members of the organization, they seem to keep slipping into technical jargon. As a result, many organizations take at face value the outputs from the R&D department and occupy themselves with the *business* impact of R&D programs. Even where performance improvement and reengineering projects introduced to the rest of the organization have also been applied to R&D, a void between the business units and the technologists still seems to exist. This gap has its roots in understanding what R&D really means to the firm.

For some years now, there has been a lot of debate about

the distinction between research (R) and development (D). That debate has tended to focus on whether companies should do a small amount of research (r) and a lot of development (D), or a lot of research (R) and a small amount of development (d). The discussion is quite unnecessary and misleading. The point is that R&D has to be managed.

RESEARCH SHOULD BE THE DOMAIN OF ACADEMICS

There appear to be two distinct types of R. The first is academic R, which, as its name implies, is essentially driven through universities and other research-type institutes. The objective of this type of work is to push back the frontiers of technology and knowledge. It has a very important role in how mankind, as a species, develops in the future. However, there are no limits on where research can lead, and, more important, there are no tangible goals or outputs. No industrial organization should be undertaking this work within its own R&D organization. If it feels philanthropic, it can fund universities or institutes, but even so, it should specify some form of return from the investment. Essentially, any "investment" in academic research should be regarded as dead money since the odds on its delivering any return to the business may be considered the same as those of winning a national lottery.

Many organizations proudly say that they undertake no academic research but that they do industrial research. This may simply disguise the problem described above, as there are two kinds of industrial research. The first is often referred to as *basic industrial research* and, in many ways, is similar to academic research. It purports to be pushing the limits of knowledge and technology in the specific industry sector in which the firm operates. Again, the main problem is that few requirements are demanded of it in terms of delivering bottom-line benefit to the organization. It is an activity more appropriately contracted out to universities, technology institutes, or contract research organizations.

The second type of industrial research is often referred to as *applied research*. The term implies that there is a goal or a defined set of outputs from the research, since it *applies* to that sector or industry. All too often, however, within the R&D organization itself, far too much effort and resource is wasted following basic tracks of research that will, in all probability, have very little impact on the bottom line of the business. It is an intellectually challenging set of tasks that the researcher comes to work to do each day. The crime for the organization, however, is that those undoubted talents are not being effectively applied to the benefit of the company and its shareholders.

THE WHOLE SPECTRUM OF DEVELOPMENT IS THE DOMAIN OF IN-HOUSE MANAGEMENT

Development, on the other hand, has a much more fundamental role to play in contributing to the success of the company. If a company has a development group that is applying scientific, engineering, or technological knowledge in a *systematic* way to improve performance, it can start thinking about going for growth and increasing shareholder value.

However, just as there is no standard definition of the term *research,* there is no common agreement, at times even within a firm, on what is meant by *development.* One approach is to consider it as a set of activities that will deliver a *balanced portfolio* of derivative, next-generation, and breakout products. *Derivative products* are those that incorporate incremental improvements, brought about by improving the manufacturing process or component assembly, for example, to reduce the cost of delivering products to the market. *Next-generation products* are those that are either significantly cheaper for the customer, with the same functionality, or those with significantly more functionality at the same cost. *Breakout products* represent a breakthrough in the application of technologies that significantly differentiates them from anything that currently exists—for example, the introduction of compact discs to replace cassette tapes and vinyl records.

Having understood the differences between research, development, and product breakout (which are discussed further in Chapter 2), the chief executive is now in a position to question what is happening within her or his own R&D organization.

MAXIMIZING RETURNS FROM THE BUSINESS AND TECHNOLOGY STRATEGIES

In every firm, the chief executive must define in clear and unambiguous terms the direction in which the firm is moving. This direction is reflected in the business strategy, and each subset of the organization can then put together its own plans in support of the strategy. It is incumbent upon the chief executive of any major telecommunications equipment supplier, for example, to have a vision of the markets that the company is going to attack and succeed in, given the significant changes taking place in the telecommunications sector around the world. For any telecommunications equipment supplier to state that it will have a presence in *all* fixed and mobile communications markets worldwide is a virtually impossible challenge. To set a vision and define a strategy to become the world leader in the supply, installation, and, perhaps, maintenance of mobile communications networks, while still a daunting task, at least sets some boundaries for the organization and for R&D.

Having defined overall business direction and strategy, the chief executive has a major role to play in managing individual units to ensure that marketing, operations, and financial performance are moving in the right direction. Just as important is to ensure that the technology direction of the business is supporting the overall business strategy.

It is a fact of life that many firms whose futures are dependent on the application of an increasingly diverse range of technologies are led by senior managers with a very limited understanding of the major technological opportunities or risks that are addressed every day within their organizations. Too few firms are exploiting their technological competencies and capabilities to the maximum. Too few firms really know how to exploit, in the marketplace, their capital in intellectual property rights (IPR). Too many firms waste time and money on expensive legal resources and processes to "protect" IPR rather than driving value out of existing investments. Too many firms measure expenditure on R&D as a percentage of sales rather than its impact on growth (or a fall) in profits.

It is the chief executive's responsibility to question, at regular intervals, how the technology strategy is being developed and integrated with the rest of the business. This can be done by regularly reviewing how the portfolio of products is being planned and managed as well as assessing other key activities including the impact of technology developments and futures, scenario planning, and the like. R&D projects should be categorized as derivatives of current products, as next-generation products—for example, a smaller, cheaper, higher-functionality mobile handset—or as breakout innovative products, perhaps integrating voice and video services within a common handset.

Achieving this balance within the portfolio is extremely difficult, but not impossible. Many iterations should take place within the process to integrate the business and technology strategy. The subelements of both strategies, including markets, financing, technical risk, competition, regulations, and so on, all come into play. The organization can use either empirical knowledge to develop the overall business plans in support of the strategy, and/or business simulation modeling techniques to help evaluate the complex linkages between the different parts of the business systems. It is the chief executive's responsibility then to oversee the execution of the fused strategy.

Since the work that R&D does is so fundamentally important to the business, firms must be convinced that the whole process is delivering measurable value. They therefore need to get much better at *assessing* the value that R&D can add. Of course, there will always be risk associated with technology, and while it is impossible to eliminate the uncertainty of the future, R&D and the other functions, including marketing and production, must be committed to a process of rigorously and continuously analyzing the valuation of key projects that are embedded in the business strategy.

Option modeling enables managers to make better decisions by incorporating the value of their ability to make *future* decisions. It solves both the complexity problem and the valuation of options in the same process by combining option-pricing theory and risk analysis, using simulation techniques. Combining these processes generates models for valuing R&D decisions that preserve the information about uncertainty and reflect the values of options to make choices in the future. The whole subject of how returns from the business and technology strategies can be maximized is contained in Chapter 3.

PICKING THE TECHNOLOGY WINNERS AND MANAGING RISK

The chief executive of a major electronics company, questioned recently about the most important business issues for him and his two-billion-dollar organization, said that his first major concern was how he could continue to improve manufacturing processes to reduce the unit cost of his major product line. This, he felt, was a task that both he and his organization were well qualified to do. The second major issue, and the one causing him the sleepless nights, was where the next major change in technology, which would either give his company a competitive advantage or give his competitors an advantage over him, was likely to occur. Essentially, every major supplier in this market, including the Japanese, is working on a breakthrough in display technology. Only one of the competing technologies is likely to find favor in the consumer and business market.

Most chief executives pride themselves on being "in tune" with what is going on in the market, but their role cannot end here. They must ensure that there is a very clear link between what the marketing department is tracking and forecasting and what is contained in the product development and innovation plans. These plans, in turn, have two key components: the link to market requirements and the identification of technology winners. The implication is that despite the fact that marketers and technologists seldom mix well, they need to work together, for together they have responsibility for the future success of the firm.

Without marketing, it is virtually impossible to assess what will and what will not be acceptable in the marketplace, yet marketing needs the contribution of the technologists to highlight the core competencies in the firm's technology base. Without R&D, marketing is not able to identify the technological trends or discontinuities that may be the foundation of new product or service opportunities. Yet tracking the technology winners cannot be left solely to the technologists, since they are not in a position to decide what is going to be most acceptable to customers in terms of price, quality, timeliness, and functionality.

Marketing departments must, however, go beyond basic market research methodologies to understand better industrial customers' buying preferences and how these can be turned into meaningful specifications that the technologists can turn quickly into winning products and services. *Customer value analysis* helps in the development of product and service strategies because it combines information on markets, competitive products, pricing, variable costs, and profit estimates to support market segmentation and decision-making on product development.

As a decision support model, it can be used by marketers to convince senior management and the technologists in R&D of the marketing benefits of changing existing products or introducing new ones. It can also raise issues relating to the introduction of new technologies to products, based on the existing core competencies within the firm. For example, if the customer value analysis identifies the potential to introduce new software features into the firm's products, what technology direction is recommended for the future?

Identifying technology winners is not a subject that the R&D department alone can address. The business as a whole must be involved when the organization bets on the next technological breakthrough. *Technology radar* is a process that will be led by R&D to evaluate the impact that evolving or new technologies will have on the firm's products or services, both near- and long-term. Confirming that the R&D department is on the right track and that it is likely to get the bet right, however, is a *management* and a *business* responsibility. Chief executives and their senior management teams must ensure that their businesses as a whole are fully briefed on what is happening in the marketplace, from marketing, technological, and competitive positioning perspectives. Under no circumstances should a business be diverted from becoming involved in the technological debate by statements from the R&D department that "everything is under control; we know what we are doing; leave us alone."

The technologists still, however, hold one trump card—the one marked "risk." Many technical projects, of course, have risk associated with them. The technologists, however, can play the card to support their own interests if senior management is not in a position to call their bluff. One of the reasons so many technical projects overrun is that senior managers do not always have the confidence to insist that the R&D budget be cut, that the project budget be cut, or even that the project be terminated.

Yet, technology risk, like any other risk, can be measured and managed. In the most technical of projects, it is not the technology itself that potentially carries the greatest risk. Given that the firm may be betting its future on the release of new products, the greatest potential threat is failing to manage that risk.

The application of techniques such as customer value analysis, technology radar, and risk analysis is helpful in defining the future product portfolio and managing delivery of the right products to the market at the right price and at the right time. Chapter 4 explains in more detail how these techniques can be applied to enhance the firm's ability to stay at least one step ahead of the competition and keep the engine of growth going.

INNOVATING TO SURVIVE

In the next millennium, the technology leaders will be those organizations that are able to manage, effectively and efficiently, the development and innovation processes for the organization. They will base their understanding of product requirements on market needs and will select the most appropriate technologies and competencies to package the products to meet those market needs. The competencies to develop the products will come either from internal resources or, as multi-technologies proliferate or technology fusion (the mixing of technologies) increases within each and every product, from the integration of internal and external competencies in product development and innovation skills.

Innovation is a word that has a lot of currency in business today, but it is a word that is not well understood. Contrary to common belief, innovation is not the exclusive domain of technologists. Anyone can come up with new ideas to improve the way the firm operates day-by-day. Innovation is more than this, however. It is the outcome of a process of product and service development, based on applying related existing market knowledge to new market applications. At the basic level, this occurs every day when one firm copies another's products or ideas. At the other end of the spectrum, real breakout opportunities, based on the introduction of new technologies, may help to secure the longer-term viability of the firm. Truly innovative firms have a culture in which good ideas are generated and the best are managed through to delivery.

Some organizations still continue with a process that started years ago, called "the suggestion box." Employees, particularly on the factory floor, were encouraged to submit suggestions for improving processes and products. If the idea was taken up, the employee was rewarded. Such schemes no longer court much favor. This may be because few firms have a continuous, rigorous, and well-managed process for assessing the real benefit to the business of *all* potentially good ideas, nor for turning ideas into tangible products and processes.

Most of the best ideas are already within the firm. Chapter 5 describes a powerful approach to innovation management which will ensure that such ideas are picked up, progressively refined, and turned into winning applications for the firm.

MANAGING THE DELIVERY PROCESS

Most chief executives, marketing directors, and finance directors understand the implications for shareholder value and cash flow of launching products and services late. Unfortunately, this knowledge is seldom translated into an increased awareness of the need to *deliver* throughout the R&D organization. Various estimates have been made of the amount of money that was lost by Microsoft in launching Windows 95 so late against the original objectives; some estimates quote over $1 billion. Eurotunnel (the rail link across the English Channel) would not be in the mess it is in today if it had been able to launch its service on its planned date rather than three years later.

Yet, as technologies proliferate, products become multi-technology-based, customers become more demanding, and the pressure for faster return on investment grows, few firms are likely to be able to survive on their own resources. The response is likely to be a growing trend toward outsourcing or setting up much more sophisticated arrangements between firms.

TO OUTSOURCE OR NOT TO OUTSOURCE?

There is a trend for more and more organizations to outsource R&D projects to other organizations, including universities and research institutes. In many cases, however, they are outsourcing low-level research, which makes no contribution to the technological leadership of the firm. In other cases, outsourcing is simply a way for the R&D organization to demonstrate that it is managing increasing numbers of projects while cutting headcount. What is actually happening, of course, is that the R&D organization is disguising its zero-increase in efficiency.

This misuse of outsourcing has to stop. Given that time to market is critical, there must be more rigor in outsourcing R&D activities to competent organizations in cases where there is pressure to deliver the product to the market earlier, where the learning curve for the new product is far too steep, or where the core competencies to develop the product do not exist within the organization.

Many external organizations have core competencies that the firm does not possess and that can be used to good effect. The starting point must be to evaluate the critical capabilities and core competencies within the firm so that decisions can be taken either to outsource key development tasks or to bring the skills in-house.

There are many examples of organizations using product development consultancies to get products to the market faster, smarter, and cheaper than their own internal organization. Although this can cause problems within the R&D organization of the firm, particularly with the "not invented here" syndrome, external organizations can often look at problems in a much more open and innovative way and come up with the solutions in a more timely manner. Most contract consultancies cannot afford *not* to deliver products against specification and price because of the contractual requirements on them. The technology leaders will be those that outsource product development and product breakout in a structured and timely way.

Managing In-House Resources

Outsourcing is not the only method of filling gaps in capabilities or competencies. Setting up a virtual R&D organization is gaining acceptance as more and more firms recognize that there are major benefits, particularly in managing R&D costs and reducing time to market, in accessing the most "business-relevant" technology from the most competent sources. In a virtual R&D organization, it is likely that external resources will be providing more added value than the internal resources, as it develops a culture of technology networking, tracking, and application.

There are many rich sources of technology outside firms, even without the introduction of a virtual R&D organization. Firms should be looking to set up collaborative agreements and licensing arrangements to provide access to new technologies, guarantee new revenue streams, or speed up the development process. A firm may wish to set up joint ventures to target new streams of business where it does not have all the financial and/or development resources to proceed on its own.

For many firms, the growth strategy is predicated on merging with or acquiring other firms, with a view to acquiring a customer base or market share. It can also be undertaken to buy a technology base, but this is extremely difficult to implement effectively. This may be one reason that acquisitions are frequently shown to be value-destroying rather than value-creating.

The choice of a particular option for managing the process of delivery from R&D depends on the culture of the company, the confidence of the R&D organization, its propensity to accept change, the priorities of senior management, and the nature of the technologies the firm needs to develop. Well planned and managed, these options will provide the more entrepreneurial firms with a wider technology base to support national and international growth. They are considered in more detail in Chapter 6.

MANAGING CREATIVITY TO DELIVER TECHNOLOGY LEADERSHIP

In most R&D organizations, there is a tremendous amount of untapped creativity. At times, the scientists and technologists have difficulty articulating this creativity in ways that the rest of the business can understand, interpret, and exploit. The rest of the business therefore sometimes gets the impression that the scientific and technology community is difficult, arrogant, and out of sync with the major initiatives being pushed by the rest of the firm.

The problem with cultural differences in an organization is that they lead to different attitudes, agendas, perceptions, and influences. These, in turn, dictate differences in attitudes to authority, bureaucracy, creativity, accountability, interrelationships, and priorities. As a result, it becomes difficult to implement change, gives rise to conflict where there should be collaboration, creates misunderstandings, and suboptimizes effective and efficient working throughout the organization.

In going for growth, the firm must learn how to tap into the creativity of this unique resource by finding ways of crossing the cultural divide. The first priority is to assess how deeply any cultural divide goes. Is it based on historical events, personality clashes, a clash between personal agendas and the needs of the firm, or a clash between predilections for faultless logic and the visionary sweep?

The chief executive and his or her management team have then to decide how best to deal with it. They may choose to undertake the change program with lots of consensus, lots of team-building, the use of external consultants, and a hefty input of time and money. They may, alternatively, decide to adopt a type of control culture, making rapid changes without a long and protracted change program, as many Japanese firms do. The decision is one that only chief executives and their senior management teams can make, but it will be influenced by the current state of the business, the current potential of the R&D organization to meet the aspirations of the business, and the patience of the shareholders. Whatever their preference, however, some aspects of the cultural divide can be effectively broken down by focused technical/cultural change programs, job rotation, multifunctional teamwork on projects,* and consistent efforts at improved communications.

---

*See also Thomas W. Mullen, "Integrated Product Development—How Does It Work?" PA Consulting Group/Pugh-Roberts Associates, London, 1996.

Some organizational change may be of benefit within the R&D group. The old debate about centralized or decentralized R&D, however, is no longer relevant. Strong leadership should bring R&D into the heart of the organization, regardless of its location, and the old hierarchical constraints that have traditionally hindered efficient working should give way to the overriding needs of the business.

Leadership, of course, comes from the top, but the chief executive should have, as close adviser and confidant, an excellent chief technology officer (CTO). Together, they must have an agreed and viable plan about how R&D is going to support the firm in growing the business. The role of the chief technology officer is fundamental in this process. The CTO's knowledge of business issues should at least match his or her technology capability.

In the modified organization, line management should provide no constraints on the delivery of projects. The more advanced organizations are moving to a process where project-specific teams are set up and disbanded according to the life of the project. The flexible and learning organization is one that recognizes the strengths of its people and exploits them appropriately, to the benefit both of the firm and the individual.

How the firm can help to make R&D culturally comfortable in the organization and how it can modify the organizational arrangements to support the business's drive to growth are the subject of Chapter 7.

***

Any firm wishing to go for growth must understand that one of the most important assets that it has is its R&D organization. There must be a fundamental change in the way R&D contributes to every business if those firms that want to be technology leaders in the 21st century are to achieve their goals. A balance has to be struck between short-term development and longer-term product or service breakout if profits and cashflow are to increase this year and next year to fund longer-term projects. The firm cannot therefore leave its R&D function solely to the technologists. R&D and the general process of innovation must be managed as an asset of the firm by chief executives and their senior management teams.

The purpose of this book is to provide senior managers with insights into the mystique of R&D and how to break down this mystique and guidelines to help them exploit the untapped opportunities in R&D to deliver growth in revenues and profits. It is not a book *by* a technologist *for* technologists. The next six chapters describe the philosophy that senior managers can adopt to exploit R&D. Appendix A contains the hard guidelines for making it happen.

UNDERSTANDING THE DISTINCTION BETWEEN "RESEARCH" AND "DEVELOPMENT"

For too long, R&D organizations have been shrouded in mystery. The term itself conjures up visions of staff walking around in white coats, clutching clipboards, leaning over very complex experiments, or laboratory benches, or computer screens. The R&D organization has its own code of dress, its own code of behavior and its own methods of communication both within its own unit and, very important, with the rest of the firm. Some of today's R&D organizations are rather like the typical IT department of, say, 10 years ago. The revolution that subsequently took place there is long overdue in the R&D department.

In the early days of computing, a mystique grew up, fostered by the IT department, that computers and computer systems were very complex affairs requiring specialist attention. Users who wanted new applications were frequently regarded as a nuisance and made to feel that their requests for systems to do what they and the business needed were either unrealistic or an unnecessary burden on the IT department.

Of greater interest was the role of the IT director and the positioning of the IT department in relation to senior management. In general, the IT director reported either to the finance director or to the facilities management director, far removed from the major business decisions being taken at board level. The IT director, however, became quite adept at asking for more money to upgrade to the latest software versions, to improve the size of the machines so that they could run faster, to add to the memory capacity of the machines, or to hire more staff to expand an already burgeoning empire. IT always acknowledged that, "We haven't delivered the applications we promised (on time or within budget) in the past, but just give the department a bit more money and this time you will really see the change" or, "I know you are concerned about the cost of IT, but you really don't understand the technology, so it's not worth explaining to you where the money is going. Trust me."

The breakout from this fortress IT mentality occurred when users got access to the latest technology with PCs on their desks, and client/server networking was developed by suppliers to meet the end user's needs. About the same time, the trend to outsourcing of IT to reduce costs and deliver the benefits faster cut through all the technical mumbo-jumbo.

It is time that a similar revolution took place in R&D departments. Senior managers need to take much more of a management interest in the projects that are going on in R&D and to understand the dynamics of how development projects will deliver real financial benefits to the firm. To do this, they will have to break down the myths associated with R&D and get all of the firm's managers to drive for more product innovation and delivery.

RESEARCH IS FUNDED INSTITUTIONAL CURIOSITY

The "men in white coats" syndrome really does seem to come into play in the research environment. Even chief technology officers and R&D directors can be overawed by staff who are more interested in the intellectual challenges in their particular disciplines than in the overall benefits of what they are doing for the firm.

Allowing staff to do research is an excellent way of losing management control of an extremely important resource: the intellectual brainpower in this part of the organization. In some sectors—for example, pharmaceuticals—research is, of course, vital, but for most firms, it is a wasted and fruitless activity. Very few commercial organizations should be spending money or resources on basic or even applied research. If there is any research going on within their organizations, senior managers need to know why. They must be concerned about the R&D budget and, as a consequence, should be asking, "What are we getting for our money?" Very few ever question where all the investment in research is leading in terms of the benefit for the firm and its shareholders.

Researchers are generally much more interested in the technology, in facing the challenge in their particular field of expertise, in developing or finding out how the frontiers of technology can be pushed back, and in publishing the results of that research. They can be lauded by academia and industry alike on the pioneering work they do in their particular discipline. Over the years, some very capable technologists have carved out careers for themselves on the basis of research work they have been doing for their firms. It is probably not in their makeup, given their academic and intellectual backgrounds, to question the value of their work *for the firm*.

Of course, we should not stop all work on research. Business managers should, however, be questioning whether research should be done within the firm, at the firm's cost, and at a cost to its shareholders, so that it can be exploited elsewhere. There are so many cases of basic research undertaken by one firm and exploited by others. Xerox developed the software that was ultimately used in the Apple Macintosh. A lot of excellent research undertaken by Bell Labs (now Lucent Technologies) has been ruthlessly exploited by communications manufacturers and suppliers all over the world. The VCR and CD players are both based on science created and research undertaken in the United States, but who can name one leading U.S. manufacturer of these products? Essentially, the link between research and shareholder value is often weak or nonexistent.

Research explores basic science and is striving to increase our knowledge and push back the frontiers of science and technology. It is critical for firms to recognize that investing in research has no obvious end product or process associated with it. It is therefore extremely difficult to define when a particular piece of research has been concluded or when, if it is not showing benefit, it should be stopped.

The pursuit of more knowledge and the pushing back of the frontiers of technology is an expensive business. Even where there is no end product or process in sight, the amount of money and investment that firms make in R&D resources, computing systems, infrastructure, and facilities is frightening. Research is arguably the most costly, most complex, and least productive industrial activity that any firm can get involved in. Senior managers need to question whether they are supporting and funding institutional curiosity within their R&D organization at the expense of profits to the firm and diminished value to its shareholders.

Many organizations are now proud of the fact that they are outsourcing research. The pharmaceutical and health-care sectors, in particular, are seeing this as a more effective route to getting the process of drug development and discovery under control in terms of costs and outputs. The problem, however, is that industrial research is often outsourced for the wrong reasons, either because the proliferation of technologies means that the firm does not have all the capability in-house, or because costs are constrained and reducing headcount by outsourcing will give the appearance of reducing costs. Neither of these addresses the fundamental issue that, in general, the firm should not be investing in *any* basic research. The key to success is to exploit development and, more important, to deliver market-related products to customers faster and faster.

DEVELOPMENT IS THE EXPLOITATION OF TECHNOLOGY CREATED ELSEWHERE

Whereas research explores basic science, has no obvious end product or process, consumes large amounts of investment, and is arguably the most costly, most complex, and least productive industrial activity, development is the exploitation of technology created elsewhere. "Elsewhere" can be within the firm, within other firms, or in academia. It is much easier to manage than research, particularly if the definition of development is clear to both managers and technologists. The first important fact about development is that it has a final product or process tied to it. The development group is tasked with working on a product or process, the completion of which everyone will recognize. If the marketing department has done its job, it will be able to pass on a very clear specification of the product or process to be developed.

Development cannot succeed through product definition or specification alone, however, given the rate of change of technology and the competitive environment in which most firms now operate. One of the critical success factors in any development project, particularly if it is supporting a marketing push (as it should do), is that everybody understands the importance of time to market. Critically, the development project itself must have finite timescales to which the deliverables, as laid down in the specification, are clearly and unambiguously tied.

That, however, is not the end of the story. Marketing books are full of examples of products that were launched on the market against an agreed specification and that, at times, were even introduced to the market earlier than originally planned. This does not necessarily mean that the product will be successful. It must, of course, be priced at a level that the market will bear. Development must therefore manage its own cost base; otherwise, the price of all the products of the firm will be influenced by the overheads of running the development department. At the same time, the development department must ensure that the final product can be manufactured at a cost that is acceptable to customers.

The last part of this equation is that the end product must be targeted to provide tangible benefits for the customer. Again, the benefits can sometimes be looked at through the eyes of the development group or the marketing department. Hence, it is critical that both of these groups agree on the functional specification at the beginning of the project, ensure that the specification matches as closely as possible the market requirements, and deliver the prototype product to manufacturing. Under no circumstances should the development group be allowed to add to or subtract from the product definition, particularly where it tries to do so on the basis of, "We have been studying this new technology and we believe that it would be good to add this to the specification." Any change to the specification must be driven by business benefit and should be made only with the agreement of the marketing and finance departments.

To recap, then, development:

- Exploits technology created elsewhere
- Has a final product or process tied to it
- Has finite timescales in which to deliver
- Has finite costs for the end product
- Is targeted at tangible benefits for the customer

Achieving world-class development is a very challenging goal, and technology leaders must ensure that their development organization delivers products faster, smarter, and cheaper than their competitors. Getting the balance right is not a trivial task, as development groups are now becoming more and more involved in applying a wider range of technologies. Not so long ago, most firms could survive by having single-technology products launched onto the market. Today, most products have a plethora of technologies embedded within them and complex processes and embedded software that are necessary to drive or operate the product.

In responding to market needs, it is important to recognize that the speed of exploitation of technology is vital in terms of the profitability of the product when it is eventually launched. Many studies have shown the impact of launching a product late out of development. Figure 2-1 illustrates the percentage decrease in cumulative profit as the development of a printer is delayed and cost and quality goals are not met. The decrease in cumulative profit can be significant, sometimes in excess of 30 percent. Late delivery from development also tends to have other knock-on effects. These include quality problems, which could mean that the firm has to discount prices, or pay out on increased warranty claims, or bear development costs that are significantly higher than planned.

The total development costs and the suboptimization of the manufacturing processes can lead to significant overruns on the cost goals. The performance of development departments in delivering products on time and to budget is not impressive. In a survey of U.S. and West European companies, the Massachusetts Institute of Technology (MIT) and PA

FIGURE 2-1.   Speed of exploitation of technology is vital. (Presentation to Institute of International Research, Dallas, Texas, Battelle Memorial Institute, May 1995.)

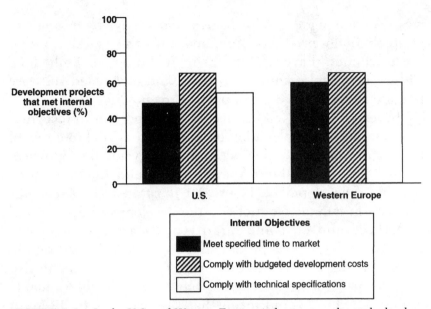

FIGURE 2-2.   In the U.S. and Western Europe, industry struggles to do development well. (MIT/PA Consulting Group Survey, 1992.)

Consulting Group analyzed the success rate of development projects in meeting the internal objectives of the firm. These objectives included tracking time to market, compliance with the original technical specification, and compliance with the budgeted development costs. The survey indicated that while Western Europe could be said to be doing marginally better than the United States (see Fig. 2-2), most development projects do not meet their internal objectives. Most worrisome, 33 percent of new industrial products launched on the market fail because the balance of time to market, specification, and costs is not achieved against the original plan.

Other surveys of UK industry undertaken by PA Consulting Group tell an even more disturbing story. Figure 2-3 shows that over 40 percent of respondents admitted that half of their internal R&D projects had overrun or overspent. In another category, over 50 percent of respondents said that recent internal projects had overrun or overspent by more than 100 percent. Nearly 70 percent of respondents had had to abandon

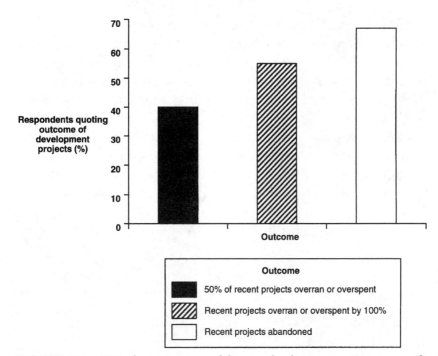

FIGURE 2-3. UK industry is poor at delivering development projects to specification. (Copyright © 1992 by the PA Consulting Group.)

recent projects because they did not have a chance of delivering against the original product specification.

Very few of these failures in development can be attributed to the technology. Comments such as, "This product is at the leading edge of technology and is therefore high-risk" should cut no ice. Why? Because the risk must be analyzed and evaluated at the beginning of the project rather than at the end or when it is abandoned. Senior managers, who are betting the financial viability of the firm on new products and services, must recognize that it is up to them to put pressure on the development department, to manage the department to deliver, and not to be fobbed off with the argument that it was the technology that was the problem.*

*See also Kenneth G. Cooper, "The $2000 Hour: How Managers Influence Project Performance," *Project Management Journal*, vol. 25, March 1994.

Of course, technology entrepreneurship, or innovation, is an important factor in beating the competition and adding value to the firm. In general, however, development activities should be focused on producing *derivatives* of products or the *next generation* of product. It should therefore be possible to manage the development process in a very structured and systematic manner, with minimal risk of the development being delivered late or over-budget. Where a product or process has to achieve an order of magnitude change in performance—probably caused by damage from competitors—or where there is a recognized need to leapfrog the competition, it is not product development that is required but product *breakout*.

PRODUCT BREAKOUT DELIVERS LEADING-EDGE APPLICATIONS OF EXISTING TECHNOLOGY

Technology leaders will be the firms that attract investment from banks, other financial institutions, and shareholders and use these funds innovatively to deliver winning technologies. They will be the firms that learn to direct and manage the intellectual capability currently residing within the R&D organization by giving those staff the challenge of providing successful outputs to the product-delivery process. These outputs need to maximize the return on the expensive funding.

Product breakout is the next step beyond product development. Product development addresses derivatives and the next generation of existing products, while the product breakout process involves much more leading-edge applications of technology. It is based on delivering "wow" products through the application of new inventions, new methods, and new ideas—but by commercially exploiting knowledge and techniques in new ways and for new purposes. The risk/reward factors in product breakout are much higher than in product development. This is where the challenge for the technologists lies.

The basic disciplines must still be adhered to. Defining a

product, assessing the costs, managing the project timescale, and clearly articulating the benefits to customers are still essential. The major difference is that the risks of *not* delivering a successful project are much higher, and, hence, there is an even greater need for closer management of the resources, timescales, and specification. Product breakout can therefore be seen at the opposite end of the spectrum from research. For the technologist, however, it can be as intellectually challenging and much more satisfying in terms of achieving something totally new and differentiated in the marketplace. Although the risks of not delivering a successful breakout product are obviously higher, the rewards can be great, too.

The Sony Walkman is one example of a breakout product. In the 1970s, Akio Morita noticed that more and more people were taking up jogging at a time when portable music was limited to transistor radios. He anticipated that consumers would love to be able to select their portable music in the same way that they could use their cassette tapes at home, hence, the creation of the portable cassette machine (Walkman), with the added bonus that it could deliver stereo sound.

The difficulty for the chief executive is trying to decide how much she or he wishes to bet the firm on investing in product breakout projects rather than straightforward product development activities, for R&D must have a balanced portfolio of products across the development and innovation spectrum.

MAXIMIZING RETURNS FROM THE BUSINESS AND TECHNOLOGY STRATEGIES

There is not a single example of a company becoming great by downsizing. Stockholders and shareholders, particularly large institutions such as pension funds, always have the option of moving their money around the global financial markets. Healthy businesses that attract investors therefore tend to be driven by chief executives whose primary aim is to increase both shareholder value[1] and the overall worth of the firm.

In going for growth, most firms are quite comfortable following the traditional routes of merging or acquiring other companies, setting up joint ventures to address particular market opportunities or needs, or simply following an organic growth strategy—expanding geographically or producing and selling more of the same products to the market. What is surprising is how little emphasis is put on growing the business through more rigorous delivery of products from R&D and exploitation of the existing technology base.

---

[1]See also Jon Moynihan, "Managing for Shareholder Value," paper series, nos. 1–8, PA Consulting Group, London, 1994; and Stephen Black, "Shareholder Value and the Sources of Business Success," PA Consulting Group, 1996.

31

The underexploitation of what, at times, are unique competencies and capabilities within the organization is a problem which impacts firms in all industry sectors. The financial institutions, particularly in some developed Western economies, such as the United Kingdom, can sometimes take a very blinkered approach to funding investments in firms to stimulate new product developments and product innovation. There is, however, a dichotomy for institutional investors when considering investing in start-up companies with no sales record or in well established companies.

Consider the case of British Biotech. It is well recognized that the need for financing high-cost, high-risk developments within the biotechnology sector is a prerequisite for bringing new drugs and medicines to the market. British Biotech, in announcing in November 1995 the preliminary results of the phase 2 trials of its anticancer drug, Marimastat—part of its drug development portfolio—increased its share price from £10 to £15 virtually overnight. Over the following months, the share price continued to climb and reached a peak of £38.25 in May 1996. Yet it will be some time before it is able to launch Marimastat on the market.

British Biotech is not unique either in the biotechnology industry or, indeed, among other industries such as software development, communications systems, and drug-delivery devices in attracting significant investment in high-risk projects. However, external investment in more mature companies, and their R&D programs, seems to be less forthcoming. Perhaps it is because their record of delivering value from R&D is so poor.

Consider the following. Figure 3-1 shows that within the top ten of the top 300 publicly listed international companies, R&D expenditure as a percentage of sales ranges from 4.5 percent for Nippon Telegraph & Telephone to 9.9 percent for Fujitsu.

This ratio of R&D expenditure to sales is often quoted by senior management in firms as a guide to their investment. As the average across the top 300 companies is 4.4 percent, firms seem to believe that investment of between 3 and 6 percent (depending on the industry sector) is a reasonable range.

FIGURE 3-1. R&D expenditure as a percentage of profit reaches alarming proportions in the world's top ten publicly listed companies

Company	Current R&D Spend Rank	Current R&D Spend $000	Sales, $M	R&D % of Sales %	R&D % of Sales Rank	Profit (Loss), $M	R&D % of Profit %	R&D % of Profit Rank
All companies composite		193,360,998	4,399,785	4.4		311,416	62.1	
General Motors, USA	1	8,373,853	168,545	5.0	150	9,758	85.8	117
Ford Motor, USA	2	6,498,099	110,310	5.9	122	3,160	205.6	38
Siemens, Germany	3	5,073,664	61,911	8.2	82	1,813	279.6	26
Hitachi, Japan	4	4,755,122	73,476	6.5	108	2,748	173.1	51
American Telephone & Telegraph, USA	5	3,711,772	79,474	4.7	159	933	397.6	12
Daimler-Benz, Germany	6	5,246,785	72,225	5.1	146	3,290	112.3	83
Mitsubishi Electric Industrial, Japan	7	3,658,965	67,243	5.4	136	2,244	163.0	55
International Business Machines, USA	8	3,381,326	71,819	4.7	159	7,799	43.4	189
Fujitsu, Japan	9	3,134,783	31,531	9.9	59	821	381.1	13
Nippon Telegraph & Telephone, Japan	10	3,038,175	68,172	4.5	166	1,644	184.7	45

Source: The UK R&D Scoreboard 1996, Company Reporting, Edinburgh, U.K., p. 52. Figures originally published in £ sterling. Conversion to $ assumes £1 = $1.55.

Note, however, that R&D expenditure as a percentage of *profit* for the same ten companies ranges from 43 percent for IBM to a staggering 397 percent for AT&T. The average across the top 300 companies internationally is 62 percent. This raises a different set of issues altogether. In particular, how long will it be before shareholders begin to question what value they are getting from this investment or, for that matter, before investors get smarter at assessing which organizations are able to get better and faster returns and growth from investment in R&D?

Not all of the investment quoted in the annual reports and accounts goes into research or applied development, of course. Significant amounts are allocated to basic engineering or process improvement activities. The point is that huge sums of money are allocated to R&D, and most firms are not maximizing the return that they get from it. Given that, in most reports and accounts, expenditure on R&D is considered to be a cost item rather than a revenue-generating part of the business, it is not surprising that the opportunities for growing the business through technology are not being exploited nearly as vigorously as they could be.

The future of many firms rests in the ability of the technologists to produce new and exciting products for the market. The one person in the firm who is responsible for unlocking this talent is the chief executive. To do this, the CEO must insist on greater integration between the business strategy and the technology strategy of the firm, then oversee the rigorous execution of that fused strategy, and constantly assure himself or herself that the whole process is delivering measurable value to the business.

FUSING THE BUSINESS AND TECHNOLOGY STRATEGIES

Perhaps one of the reasons many firms do not exploit their own technological capabilities as effectively as they could is that they are looking at the wrong model of the impact of science and technology on the business. Many senior managers still believe that basic science drives new industrial technology, which, in turn, drives firm and national economic growth. Since senior managers are often intimidated by science and technology, this growth model is not particularly appealing. In addition, they probably believe that economic growth can be fueled more effectively by increased investment from financial backers, shareholders, and so on, to drive growth through mergers and acquisitions. Indeed, this is what most business schools teach.

Future economic growth, be it by the firm or the nation, is, to an extent, dependent upon investors. However, the major driver for growth is advances in new industrial technologies.

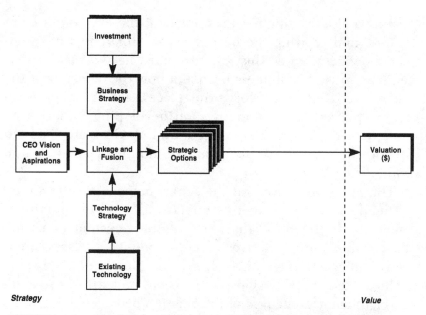

FIGURE 3-2. The link between business and technology must be exploited. (*Copyright © 1997 by the PA Consulting Group.*)

The driver for new industrial technologies is not basic science but existing and preexisting technology. A more coherent model of how business and technology interrelate is shown in Fig. 3-2 and discussed below.

Articulation of the Chief Executive's Vision and Aspirations

The chief executive's vision and aspirations for the firm are generally articulated in the strategic plan, which defines the mission of the firm; the goals, in terms of what must be achieved over time; and targets, defined by the performance levels required to meet the goals.

Formulation of the Business Strategy

The basic strategy of any firm at the highest level tends to be very clear. In essence, the business strategy can be boiled down to the key objectives of keeping existing customers, locating and attracting new customers at the expense of competitors, and growing the overall market for the firm's products or services. To do this, the firm must have a basic understanding of what customers need and how the demands of the market are being met. Most firms place a lot of emphasis on gaining market understanding and developing a marketing strategy to define which products and services are likely to provide the firm with the greatest amount of revenue and profit.

The chief executive and the senior management team are the leaders in the firm in understanding these business dynamics,[2] to the extent that they will meet customers, particularly senior representatives of key accounts, to assess their needs and assure them of the firm's commitment to add value to those customers' businesses. In some industries, there are also significant exchanges of information between competitors to increase understanding of the market and gain other business intelligence.

Senior management will also give shareholders and investors a great deal of attention. There are no problems in talking about the financial health of the firm, the development of the markets, the opportunities for increased profit, and so on. This linkage is particularly important, given that the chief executive's job is dependent on how the financial backers and shareholders assess the performance and financial health of the firm as it affects their investment.

Inputs from all of these activities are used to define the overall strategic direction of the firm. The strategy is predicated on the dynamics of the market and the perceived need for change based on these market dynamics. The most successful firms then supply the change makers in the organization with the tools and techniques to follow the strategy, and, more important, they strongly support the implementation of the

---

[2] See also James M. Lyneis, *Corporate Planning & Policy Design*, MIT Press, Cambridge, Mass., 1980. Also available through PA Consulting Group/Pugh-Roberts Associates, Cambridge, Mass.

change program to deliver the strategy. Many companies follow this process.

Formulation of the Technology Strategy

Without a doubt, technology drives industrial competitiveness. It can be a significant differentiator in the market and it can lead to increases in specification or reductions in costs for products and services, which result in major impacts on the markets and the customer base. However, technology is becoming increasingly difficult to manage because of the proliferation of technologies, shortening product life cycles, the high costs of development, and the fact that markets themselves are becoming more complex. For these reasons alone, chief executives and their senior business managers must understand what their firms' technology strategies are and what their implications are for the business.

Unfortunately, most managers today still assume that tomorrow's business will be more or less the same as today's. In particular, business managers tend to believe that major discontinuities in the market are unlikely to occur and, as a result, focus their efforts on making business operations and processes more and more cost-effective. Major discontinuities, caused by technological change and the increase in multitechnology products, are not, admittedly, easy to comprehend, and the difficulty can be exacerbated by the inability of technologists to communicate with their business colleagues.

In the 1980s, Swiss watchmakers would have followed the traditional business strategy and planning process. Why should they do anything differently? The Swiss watch industry was noted for its high-quality, well-engineered, and traditional portfolio of products. Improvements in production processes, statistical process control, and testing provided watches for the masses at what were considered (by the watchmakers) value-for-money prices. At the other end of the spectrum, high-quality, well-engineered timepieces with accuracies that would have staggered watchmakers of the seventeenth and eighteenth centuries were produced for those who could afford them. As pieces of minute mechanical engineering, the devices were astounding.

Then came new technology. The silicon chip, which was originally developed to support the computing industry, was recognized as being an ideal device to measure time. Japanese companies were able to embed within their watches tiny electronic chips that were more reliable, robust, and accurate than the mass-produced devices produced in Switzerland. Overnight, the Swiss watch industry virtually went out of business. Yet the signs were there for everyone to read.

Interestingly, the Swiss watch industry reacted in a novel way. It rationalized the industry by amalgamating several firms under the SMH banner and conceived the Swatch. This is often seen as a triumph of marketing and hype, but its real success is built on technology. New injection-moulding and welding techniques were developed for the case and glass and new, simplified manufacturing for the mechanism. The manufacturing techniques enabled an incredibly wide variety of watches to be produced without increasing the cost. In addition, SMH became the world leader in 1.5v chip technology.

These improvements in technology and manufacturing enabled the company to produce watches at a lower cost than its Asian competitors, despite Switzerland's high wage structure. Although Swatches are not as cheap as the bottom-end competition, the availability of different styles was controlled carefully, and new styles were introduced at regular intervals. By making the watch a fashion item, the company created the expectation that customers would buy to keep pace with fashion changes. Quick response in marketing and, in particular, in the application of new and innovative technologies and manufacturing processes, saved the whole industry.

In 1947, Procter and Gamble introduced the first synthetic laundry detergent, called Tide. It was a step-change improvement in performance over other washing powders because phosphates in the product increased its cleaning power. Procter and Gamble's major competitor, Lever Brothers (now Unilever), eventually launched its own product, called Surf. However, by then, its detergent market had suffered badly from the competition. In 1995, Unilever attempted to blindside Procter and Gamble with the launch of Persil Power. This contained a manganese-based additive, which, according to Unilever, would improve the washing capability of the detergent even further. Unfortunately, claims that the additive had an adverse affect on color and fibers meant that the product was not the success that the company had expected. It was withdrawn from the market in 1995. The total cost of this is variously estimated at between tens and hundreds of millions of dollars.

For any firm, therefore, it is absolutely critical to understand what is happening in R&D, if not to drive growth and provide the firm with its own ability to introduce discontinuities into the market, then at least to ensure that there are no technology "Exocets" that could have a significant negative effect on the performance of the firm. In reviewing the technology strategy, senior management must focus on the key issues of launch dates for products, risk assessments for product and service objectives, definition of resource requirements (both people and money), projected revenues in terms of when they are likely to come on stream, and compliance with what marketing expects and what production can produce. The acid test of how good the technology strategy is depends on its fit with the business strategy and its exploitation of the firm's current and future technology competencies. A review of past performance and achievement of previous objectives will provide a good indication of whether the technologists really have the potential to deliver benefit for the business.

LINKING THE STRATEGIES

Senior management and, in particular, the chief executive, must ensure that there is an overt and powerful link between the business strategy and the technology strategy. This is not to say that the overall business strategy cannot have a technology push. It is, however, imperative that if the chief executive and senior managers have decided on a particular strategic direction for the firm, the technologists must be working on projects that support that strategy.

The chief executive can ensure coherency and consistency among the technologists and the nontechnologists by insisting that:

- The technology strategy is formulated in a language that senior managers and other business managers understand.
- There are explicit linkages between the technical strategy and the business strategy in terms of how markets are to be addressed by the products emerging from R&D.
- The technology projects show clear linkages with the business plans, not just in terms of the technology base of the products but, as important, in terms of the linkages to projected revenue streams.
- All R&D projects within the technology strategy have well-defined budgets and project deliverables.
- There is a balanced portfolio of projects[3] covering derivatives, next-generation, and breakout projects.

The last of these is probably the single most important factor in linking the business and technology strategies. R&D must have a portfolio that covers the spectrum, from projects producing short-term benefits to longer-term breakout projects with major promise.

SELECTING STRATEGIC OPTIONS

Each strategic option for the portfolio should be considered. Hidden away in most R&D organizations are projects that the technologists and scientists consider to be "strategically important." They tend to have lives of their own, either because the project has been running for so long that nobody will admit that it is a rogue that needs to be killed off or because the technology challenge is so strong that it has become a pet pro-

---

[3]See also David R. Shinkfield and Kenneth G. Cooper, "The Pharmaceutical Portfolio—Navigating an Uncertain Future," *Scrip Magazine*, November, 1994; and John Marriage, "Portfolio Management—The Route to Innovation Led Growth," PA Consulting Group, London, 1996.

ject within the R&D organization. Significant resources are frequently wasted on such projects, with a highly detrimental effect on the overall efficiency and effectiveness of R&D.

The options selected are those that will have maximum impact on the revenues and profits of the firm. Option modelling and dynamic business simulation models help to define which projects are likely to deliver, in what timescale.

DRIVING THE PRODUCT DEVELOPMENT AND BREAKOUT PROCESS

Once the strategic options have been defined, the hard work really starts—delivering products. The execution phase (Fig. 3-3)

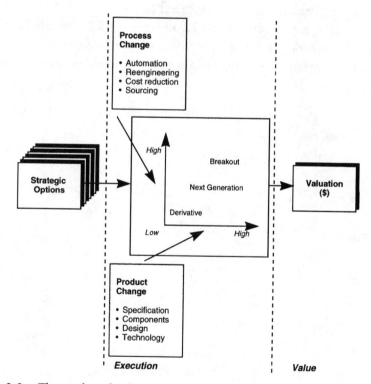

FIGURE 3-3. The product development and breakout process requires close collaboration between marketing, production, and R&D. (*Copyright © 1997 by the PA Consulting Group.*)

requires very close working between marketing, production, and R&D. R&D should have a continual process for reviewing all ongoing projects. The chief technology officer and his or her team should be at least one step ahead. They should be looking through the full portfolio of product development and innovation projects, defining them in terms of whether or not they are going to deliver derivative, next-generation, or breakout products. These clearly have to be linked to the overall business strategy.

In reviewing the product portfolio, it is likely that R&D will identify some projects that fall in the low-risk and high-reward category. These should be brought to the attention of marketing to assess whether they should be included in the overall portfolio (Fig. 3-4). Projects that are high-risk and low-return should be killed off immediately. The high-reward, low-risk projects should be exploited fast.

Most R&D organizations have well-defined product-development processes with gating procedures at each stage of the development of a new product. The problem seems to be that

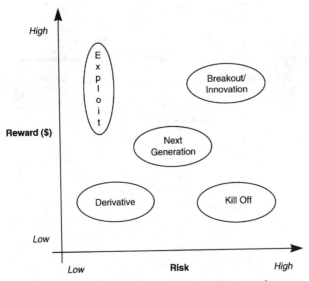

FIGURE 3-4. The development portfolio must be managed to maximize returns. (*Copyright © 1997 by the PA Consulting Group.*)

once a project is launched, it can take on a life of its own within the R&D organization. Regular reviews of progress against original objectives, assessment of the market dynamics, and total openness on the expenditure of the R&D resources (money and manpower) should be high on the agenda of the regular management meetings. Where projects are slipping, and revenue is thus bound to be lost, questions must be asked and actions taken to correct shortfalls in project deliverables. There should be no surprises with any of the key R&D projects.

The impact on the technologists is that their value and worth to the firm should become more and more evident to everyone. They should be regarded as revenue generators, not as cost overheads. Their input to process improvements in manufacturing, their ability to spot new technological changes, and their ability to deliver new products based on improved specifications and the applications of new technologies should be valued by the whole firm.

DELIVERING BUSINESS VALUE FROM TECHNOLOGY

There is an old adage, "If you can't measure it, you can't manage it." Within most R&D organizations, there is also a belief that you cannot manage creativity too closely or measure it too critically. Both points of view have a ring of truth, but since the work that R&D does is so fundamentally important to the business, firms need to get much better at assessing the value that R&D can add.[4] In all walks of life, complexity and uncertainty prevail. In trying to value R&D projects, it is impossible to eliminate the uncertainty of the future. However, this is not a good reason for failing to follow a

---

[4]See also John Marriage, "How to Measure the Business Value of Innovation," PA Consulting Group, London, 1996; and Stephen Black, "Accounting for R&D," PA Consulting Group, 1996.

process to improve decision making. Various options are in common use:

- Conventional discounted cash flow (DCF) approaches tend to combine corrections for inflation, the time value of money (based on how much a firm can make from a zero-risk investment), and the "riskiness" of the project cash-flows. These are lumped together to give a single discount rate. This has some convenience value but can have very bad side effects, because a single discount rate may render the technique poor to worse-than-useless for high-risk or long-term investments.

- An alternative is to separate out the risk and incorporate probability weightings into cashflow to give "expected values." This method has the advantage that it makes risk visible rather than burying it in arguments about "hurdle" rates. Its disadvantage is that there are no explicit decision points to help assess the value of projects.

- A business model can be used to run scenarios, with different values for each variable. However, if each variable has a number of discrete values, the number of scenarios that have to be reviewed to capture all the possible outcomes quickly rises to a very significant and daunting number. Very few managers in firms are able to deal with the complexity of such scenario developments or evaluations and are therefore not able to come to sensible decisions on the basis of such analysis.

Given all the variables in any R&D project—the targeted product price, the cost of manufacture, the time-to-launch, the resource requirements in R&D, and capital expenditure—better ways have to be found to undertake a valuation on which decisions can be made that go beyond the methods described above.

A useful approach is to solve both the complexity problem and the valuation of options in the same process by combining option-pricing theory and risk analysis, using simulation techniques. Combining these processes can generate models for valuing R&D decisions that preserve the information about uncertainty and reflect the values of options to make choices in the future. The approach involves building future decisions into a spreadsheet model of the business by using simple decision rules. The process can also use ranges rather than single numbers to incorporate knowledge about key uncertainties. It is then possible to calculate a large number of scenarios from a statistically meaningful selection of the inputs. The output of this is a forecast with a range of values of the projects. This process is called *option modelling*.

Option modelling provides firms with a simplified presentation of what they already know. It achieves this while embodying more information than is typically presented using other techniques, and without simplifying or neglecting interactions between the different uncertainties in alternative scenarios. Its advantages over other methods include:

- The output from option modelling preserves both the value and the risk estimates and keeps them separate, enabling management to do much better portfolio analysis where they are considering multiple projects.

- It is interactive, so it can be used to model the results of alternative decision strategies. Through such sensitivity analysis, managers may get a better idea of which areas of uncertainty to focus on, for example, or of where greater value can be created by rearranging the priorities of R&D stages.

- Option modelling can focus attention on how best to manage the risks inherent in a single project. If, for example, the biggest unknown is market size, it would be wise to focus some attention on market research before committing vast sums to solving the technical problems. Or perhaps a pilot-scale, low-risk product needs to be launched to test market reaction before committing large levels of investment.

Alternatively, the manufacturing process needs to be developed concurrently with product development because the firm may be able to develop the product but not produce it in a cost-effective way.

- It is an aid to managing risk at the portfolio level as well as at the project level. The risks that really matter to management are the risks of the total portfolio of R&D projects, for it must judge the overall returns from R&D investment, not whether an individual project will succeed. For example, it is easy to show that attempts to "improve" the returns that R&D provides by stopping the highest-risk projects can actually reduce the value of the portfolio.

- Senior management needs to take an intelligent view of the sources of risk in each project so it can manage the R&D portfolio risk to an acceptable degree, even when many projects have very high individual risks. For example, if an oil company bets all its development projects on a rising oil price, that is a high risk. If, however, it has a portfolio of development projects, some of which depend on a rising price and some of which depend on a falling price, its portfolio is of low risk even though each project is highly dependent on unpredictable circumstances. Option modelling quantifies risk separately from financial value, so it is possible to use the output to make value/risk trade-offs in portfolio modelling.

R&D and the other business units, including marketing and production, must be committed to a process of rigorously and continuously analyzing the valuation of key projects that are embedded in the business strategy. Any form of modelling that enables managers to make better decisions by incorporating the value of their ability to make *future* decisions must be of benefit to the firm.[5]

[5]See also Lyneis, 1980.

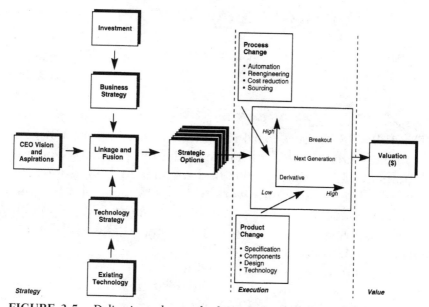

FIGURE 3-5. Delivering value to the business starts with a vision and ends with execution. (*Copyright © 1997 by the PA Consulting Group.*)

* * *

The process described in this chapter can be illustrated as a generic business and technology model (see Fig. 3-5). It starts with the chief executive's vision and aspirations, which are then fused, by the CEO and senior management team, with the business and technology strategies of the firm. This fusion results in the definition of a series of strategic options. They are critically evaluated to assess their bottom-line impact. The best options define the product portfolio. The worst are killed off.

The product and service portfolio, critically evaluated and reported on at regular intervals, is then project-managed to delivery. Post-delivery, projects are re-evaluated to check what was really delivered in terms of shareholder value, and the results and lessons are fed back into the option evaluation process.

Sounds easy? Then why do so many firms spend more on R&D than they make in profit?

CASE STUDY—GENERAL MOTORS

Dare to dream, dare to be wrong, dare to be leaders...

Ken Baker

Vice President R&D, General Motors

The 1996 R&D Scoreboard Report, sponsored by the UK government's Department of Trade and Industry, lists General Motors (GM) as the number one spender of R&D funds for publicly listed companies worldwide.* On sales of $164 billion, GM made a profit of $4.9 billion. It spent $8.9 billion on Research, Development, and Engineering (R,D,&E). (Figures taken from GM annual report, 1996.)

There are three interesting points to note about this funding of R&D. First, the vast majority of it is spent not on what is traditionally known as R&D but on engineering to develop new processes, new models, and investments to continuously improve manufacturing techniques. Second, this total expenditure of R&D and engineering budget is bigger than many companies quoted in the scoreboard report achieve in sales! A third surprising point is that dollars spent on actual R&D represent a fraction of the total R,D,&E budget. As a consequence, R&D funding must be apportioned and managed wisely if it is to have directional impact on business value creation.

The ups and downs of the boardroom and business activities of GM have been documented in many other books and publications. What happened in the past cannot be changed; however, in terms of the future, it is clear that GM as a major automobile manufacturer is at a crucial stage in the development of its business.

Like many automobile and truck manufacturers, GM faces a major threat from Japanese competition, even in the loyal heartland of its Midwestern markets. In addition, GM has to

---

*source: The UK R&D Scoreboard 1996, Company Reporting, Edinburgh, UK, p. 52. Figures originally published in £ sterling. Conversion to $ assumes £1 = $1.55.

cope with a change in attitude by younger buyers to seek value for money and differentiation in automobile products.

Much of GM's early success was due to a strong emphasis on product and process innovation. Many of these innovations were introduced under the management of "Boss" Kettering, head of R&D at GM from 1920 to 1947. Boss Kettering was, and still is, regarded as one of the most innovative and exciting engineers of his time. However, the lead that GM established during this golden era has come under intense pressure from a host of worldwide competitors. As a result, today the organization is working hard to resurrect its legacy and indeed improve upon it.

A pivotal change came in 1993 when Ken Baker, who came to the R&D group from the operating side of the firm, was appointed Vice President of R&D for GM's automotive division. Ken's background as an engineering manager was considered a plus even though, as he explains (and not defensively) in terms of science qualifications within his R&D group, he is well down the ladder. Ken's experience in operations was considered by top management to be just what was needed to meld GM's R&D group into its business operations. He came to R&D with a clear mandate from GM's business leadership to reinvigorate the development and innovation processes within GM.

When Baker took over in 1993, he was faced with an R&D group that had a budget of approximately 0.11 percent of total revenues of the automotive and truck divisions. Fifty-five percent of staff had been cut back in the previous seven years and budgets for R&D had been cut by 50 percent over the same period. In his own words, "R&D in GM at that time was an academic- and scientific-based institution. Core competency was based on scientific discipline, not the ability to create shareholder value."

Baker started by reviewing current projects and, most important, the people within the R&D organization. Very early on, he recognized that the future, in terms of development of products for GM, was uncertain and that it was inappropriate for R&D on its own to try to predict the future. However, it was imperative that a program be put in place to balance the short-term business needs of GM with the longer-term (10 to 15 years) technical needs envisioned for the full range of automotive products.

Ken Baker's plan was to achieve a transition from a very traditional R&D environment to a state where R&D could be categorized as a learning enterprise focused both on the needs of its internal customers (the business units within GM), and the end customer (the buyer of the GM car or truck) for the near term and in the future. In 1993 he introduced programs to focus R&D on recognizing that it had to become more customer driven. In 1994 the emphasis was on strengthening the global position of R&D as a key enabler within GM as a whole. The focus in 1995 was to make R&D a business sector within GM where it could create substantial business opportunities for the company, a key factor being to move R&D from being a cost overhead to being revenue generating.

As part of the ongoing development of R&D as a business, Baker examined how new business practices could be introduced to the organization. This involved achieving increased understanding of customer standard values and developing new ways of conducting the R&D business. In addition to working more closely with the individual business units, this included exploiting the intellectual capital within the organization, to attract funds either from within GM or from collaborative arrangements and partnerships with other organizations. For Baker, the leveraging of new business was one of the ways to generate additional funding that could be ploughed back into the development of new ideas to the benefit of GM.

The change program introduced within the R&D organization required two major changes in culture. Fundamentally, Baker undertook what he terms "a root-and-branch evaluation of our core competencies," deciding that what was needed was a very clear and unambiguous evaluation of what was essential to the business so that the customer would get what he wanted. Most important, it was necessary to ensure that the competition did not have access to the patents and intellectual property in which GM intended to invest.

From this process came a list of core competencies which are going to be built on for the future of GM and its shareholders. They include:

- Advanced propulsion technology based on traditional and new methods of propulsion (including electric vehicles)
- Advanced body technology
- Vehicle optimization
- Organizational ability to undertake change and to exploit new technologies rapidly and with the maximum amount of quality

Baker then decided that R&D had to be organizationally interdependent, based on a redefinition of the skills of its scientists and engineers. As a result, R&D was reorganized around the core competencies defined by an external consultancy and the needs of internal and external customers. This was a radical move away from the original organizational structure based on chemists, metallurgists, and engineers grouped together by scientific and engineering disciplines. "The original grouping was not the way to develop innovative processes," says Baker. "It was important to get people thinking outside their own box."

The final change he made was to add production capability into R&D. This essentially was to move away from the traditional method of developing new products based on isolation of R&D from production to one where everyone in R&D and production could increase their confidence in being able to change traditional behaviors to provide what the market wants and when it wants it. The teams in R&D are now responsible for delivering from concept through to implementation.

The ongoing strategy of "Jack" Smith, chief executive of GM, is similar to that of many chief executives of leading organizations: growth in revenues, growth in profits, and growth in GM's global business in the automotive sector. Smith has said that he believes that the role of R&D is vital in supporting these ongoing strategic business intents of the company, and, as a result, Ken Baker is aligning the R&D organization along three overlapping groupings:

Customers	who are becoming more demanding in their requirements for improved safety, higher reliability, and improved quality.
Society	where increasing pressure is being put on automotive manufacturers to design cars and trucks that are environmentally friendly and more efficient in their use of energy. For example, GM is working on processes to improve fuel efficiency by a factor of three at an affordable price.
Enterprise	where the demands of the firm are also taken into account. An example of this is support for the globalization process within GM.

As far as the future is concerned, Baker believes that any leading R&D organization "must be able to deal with discontinuous change—by being fast, focused, and flexible. Although the emphasis is on growth for the firm, all R&D organizations should operate in a continuous TQM and reengineering mode." In this way he believes that the portfolio of current projects should be regarded as exercisable options which R&D and other business units can decide to cash in or not. "Fundamental in developing the concept of exercisable options is recognition that the traditional role of R&D in sitting back and waiting for the customer to come to them does not work."

The new way of doing R&D within GM is a business approach. The innovation process has been formalized within a business framework through which the global acquisition, prioritization, and deployment of technology development is managed. Within the business framework the R&D portfolio of projects is regularly re-evaluated, using a decision process that includes dialogue with key "stakeholders" within the organization. R&D department heads are assigned as technical liaisons to internal operating customers. Innovation teams are made up of R&D, operational, and marketing representatives. Most important, top GM business and technical managers set the directional trends for R&D within GM. In summary, the innovation process involves everyone in innovation projects—from senior GM management right down to the release engineer.

Certainly Baker believes that the head of R&D plays a major role in formulating the vision of the enterprise and where it will go in the future. "R&D must earn the right to become a more valued resource," he says. "The CEO must feel comfortable about the R&D portfolio and that it is worth investing in. The portfolio must have the right balance of enhancements to current projects as well as identifying new business opportunities. These business opportunities should be based on the premise that they can be venture capital investments internal to the firm. The strategic intent of the company must be driven by the CEO and the Board, but it is then a management imperative to ensure that the R&D portfolio matches this intent and is worth investing in."

Ken Baker has undoubtedly made significant changes to the R&D organization within GM. However, these changes have not been easy to implement and are only the start of the process to move the world's leading vehicle manufacturer to a position where it can once again claim also to be the world's automotive technology leader. Just as "Boss" Kettering worked hand-in-glove with GM's legendary chairman Alfred P. Sloan, Jr., to establish the company's remarkable record of early innovative success, today Ken Baker is working closely with Jack Smith and GM senior management to reestablish that innovative heritage. Only time will tell whether Baker can help GM successfully emulate the Sloan-Kettering record of achievement, but his is the hand guiding GM's R&D efforts into the next century and his efforts are of fundamental importance to the future success of the company.

PICKING THE TECHNOLOGY WINNERS AND MANAGING THE RISK

There are two major requirements for picking technology winners. The first is understanding the opportunities in the marketplace. The second is ensuring that the firm can detect and exploit those opportunities with the timely application of new technologies. Both requirements are fundamentally important in ensuring that firms launch products in a timely fashion so as to exploit the window of opportunity in the market. Two powerful techniques are available to help companies with these tasks. *Customer value analysis* helps to define the market opportunities. *Technology radar* helps to identify winning technologies, as they apply to a particular firm and its competencies.

However, any process that requires analysis of the market and an assessment of the evolution of technology to meet future market needs is risky. Senior managers have to accept that market and technology discontinuities will occur, and they have to learn to manage risk. To not do so is an abrogation of managerial responsibility.

CUSTOMER VALUE ANALYSIS HELPS TO DEFINE MARKET OPPORTUNITIES

In many functional organizations, decisions relating to product development are typically first addressed in the marketing department. Discussions may often be limited to marketing's area of responsibility, without any account being taken of other aspects of product development, including R&D and manufacturing. As a result, an imprecise and risky market and financial case may be put before senior management. The problem for the marketers is that marketing is not an exact science, and, probably more troublesome, most senior managers in the firm believe intuitively that they know what the market wants.

Market research techniques have become more powerful and much more sophisticated, but it is still difficult to convince senior management on the basis of market information alone. In particular, in an increasingly competitive environment, it is important to offer products and services that not only fulfil customers' needs but that also optimize the profits for the company in the long term. This means that products and services must be aligned with the core competencies that the firm's R&D organization can deliver and that its factories can manufacture.

Often, products are evaluated on the basis of their expected impact on market share, on the assumption that this is going to be a profitable development for the firm. This approach is doubly flawed. First, a product that the customer wants might be so expensive for the business to develop or to manufacture that it would be impossible to make any profit. Second, a presumed increase in market share alone is not a valid measure; in a growing market, it is possible to maintain a given sales level even though market share falls.

Figure 4-1 shows the relationship between market share and profit per unit sold. It is clear from the figure that measures that move the product or service up and to the right are positive, whereas measures that move the product down and

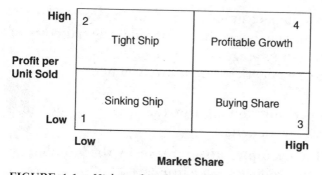

FIGURE 4-1. High market share and high profit per unit sold drives profitable growth. (*Copyright © 1997 by the PA Consulting Group.*)

to the left are negative. However, the net effect on the bottom line of measures that move the product to the right and down or to the left and up is not intuitive. What is required is a systematic approach to assessing the market potential of alternative product decisions.

In the customer value analysis process, a market simulation model is developed to assess the wants and needs of customers. In individual interviews, samples of existing and potential customers are asked questions that require them to make trade-offs between product features, based on their personal preferences and values. The output of the interview is an individual decision model that can be used to predict how this customer will react to different product offerings in the marketplace.

Many such individual decision models are then aggregated into a market simulation model, where the competitive arena for the industry can be simulated and the market potential for existing or new products can be analyzed. The main drivers that affect market potential, such as physical product features, price, service level, and distribution, are included in this simulation model.

On its own, this process will not convince senior management that the answers are any different from those deriving from normal market research techniques. What will convince them is seeing the impact on costs of changing existing products or introducing new ones, that is, the differential costs of alternative product or strategy decisions.

There are three categories of cost involved here:

- Variable cost per unit volume (for example, a change to a more expensive raw material)
- Fixed cost (for example, an increase in the number of employees in the production department)
- Investment cost (for example, investment in a new assembly line for a new product)

The strategy discussion can be enhanced by a decision support model, which consists of three elements, an optimization model, a market simulation model, and a financial model. These are illustrated in Fig. 4-2 and discussed below.

- *The Optimization Model:* Here, market information collected in the interviews is combined with financial information relating to alternative product decisions. The optimization process (using linear programming techniques) finds

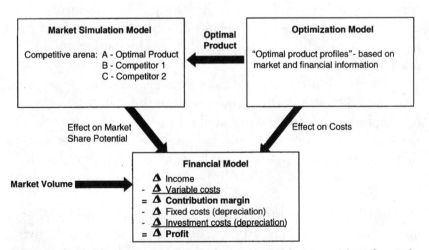

FIGURE 4-2. The customer value analysis supports decision making for product and service strategy. (*Copyright © 1997 by the PA Consulting Group.*)

product profiles that are popular in the marketplace and that have a cost structure that makes it possible for the firm to make a profit. Investment and fixed costs are not included in the optimization, the focus being on the marginal, variable costs per unit produced.

- *The Market Simulation Model:*   When an "optimal product" profile is found, that product can be input to the market simulation model to analyze the effects of cannibalization, for example, where the new product takes market share from the company's own product. The optimization model and market simulation analyses use an iterative process so optimization criteria, based on outputs from the market simulation model, can be changed to produce even better product profiles. The market simulation model can then be run for simulation on *segments* to see how different customer groups react to new product introductions.

- *The Financial Model:*   The output from the market simulation model, expressed as changes in market share potential, can be combined with information on market volume to assess either the total market or the market for particular segments. This provides information on the income side of the new product introduction.

The cost structure relating to a particular product profile can then be introduced to analyze the bottom-line effect of the new product. Alternative product profiles are then presented in a consistent format. As a result, projects can be evaluated and prioritized based on their contribution to bottom-line output for the business unit. Qualitative indicators for assessing risk can also be included, covering, for example, how difficult it would be to implement different product features.

A major European airline, suffering from invasive competition in its previously highly regulated local market, applied the approach with startling results. The analysis revealed that the airline was neglecting its core business, believing that its customers wanted more on-board extras when, in fact, what most influenced customers' buying decisions was speed through the airport and flight punctuality.

TECHNOLOGY RADAR HELPS TO DEFINE THE WINNING TECHNOLOGIES FOR A FIRM

Technology radar helps a firm to make decisions about the products that it provides to the market by evaluating the impact that technology will have on those products. It can be broad enough in scope to be of value to corporate decision makers and business unit leaders in product planning and process development. It can also be sufficiently detailed and focused to help the R&D department undertake technological assessments at a level that will meet its scientific and engineering requirements, set targets for projects, and control the R&D budget. It is, in addition, a powerful metaphor that engages the interest and enthusiasm of business units as well as the R&D department.

Managing the cross-functional involvement in an active technology research program such as this requires constant consultation, transparent communication, and a common language. The development of a common language primarily helps the business units to understand the technological aspects of the program and stops the research from getting too deeply bogged down in "technospeak." However, the technical staff will probably need assistance in carrying out active market-facing research and will require training and enthusiastic support from their line management. The assistance of the business unit managers in helping them make this transition can break down the cultural barriers between the R&D organization and the other units.

The concept of technology radar, using military metaplans (see Fig. 4-3), is that a firm must be able to detect the changes that will occur in the technological landscape over time and assess their impact on its overall strategic and tacti-

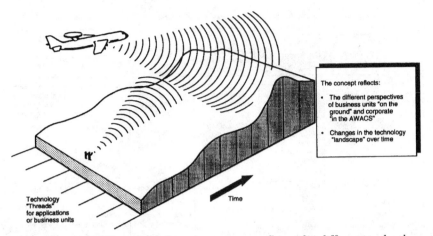

FIGURE 4-3.   The technology radar concept reflects the different technology perspectives within the firm. (*Copyright © 1997 by the PA Consulting Group.*)

cal business (battle) plan. At any one time, a firm will be following, or needs to pursue, several technological "threads"— for specific applications in a technological sense, or for business units in their respective business environments. The concept reflects the fact that there are different perspectives for business units, based "on the ground," and for corporate, which could be considered to be embodied over the horizon by the early warning "AWACS."

The overall process is defined in Fig. 4-4. It consists of three main phases. However, given that it takes a lot of time and resources to produce meaningful results, it is critical to reactivate the technology radar process regularly, probably on an annual basis, to ensure that it is continually refined and enhanced. This is the same process as developing a database of key information, to keep it continually refreshed and up-to-date.

CALIBRATION OF THE RADAR

The first task is to define the firm's needs and check that the technology radar is properly "calibrated." To calibrate the radar, the firm must generate specific intelligence requests, containing a statement of the management decisions requiring fund-

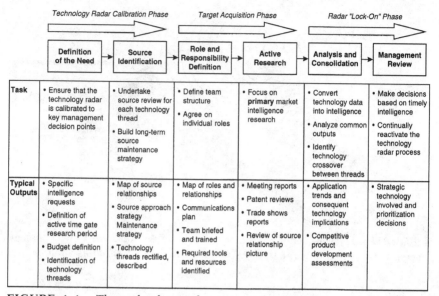

	Technology Radar Calibration Phase	Target Acquisition Phase	Radar "Lock-On" Phase

	Definition of the Need	Source Identification	Role and Responsibility Definition	Active Research	Analysis and Consolidation	Management Review
Task	• Ensure that the technology radar is calibrated to key management decision points	• Undertake source review for each technology thread • Build long-term source maintenance strategy	• Define team structure • Agree on individual roles	• Focus on **primary** market intelligence research	• Convert technology data into intelligence • Analyze common outputs • Identify technology crossover between threads	• Make decisions based on timely intelligence • Continually reactivate the technology radar process
Typical Outputs	• Specific intelligence requests • Definition of active time gate research period • Budget definition • Identification of technology threads	• Map of source relationships • Source approach strategy Maintenance strategy • Technology threads rectified, described	• Map of roles and relationships • Communications plan • Team briefed and trained • Required tools and resources identified	• Meeting reports • Patent reviews • Trade shows reports • Review of source relationship picture	• Application trends and consequent technology implications • Competitive product development assessments	• Strategic technology involved and prioritization decisions

FIGURE 4-4. The technology radar process consists of three main phases. (*Copyright © 1997 by the PA Consulting Group.*)

ing and resources and the objectives that will be served by the decisions in terms of product outputs and market to be addressed. This can be done in terms of the context and the timescales in which the decision must be taken, for example, how soon and how much of a return the firm expects from new technology applications. In particular, the scope of the radar search must be defined in terms of scan *width* (breadth of technologies to be considered), scan *time gate* (the time ahead that the scan needs to cover), business options, dependencies, and assumptions. It is useful to include here a requirement to scan for potential technology "Exocets," that is, emerging technologies that have the potential to knock out the established players or otherwise affect the firm's intentions.

Typical outputs from this activity include the specification of technology requests and information requirements and the time period in which the information is to be collected. The particular technological threads can be as broad or as deep as required. However, in integrating the business and technological strategies, the greatest value is derived when there is agreement on which threads need to be identified and tracked. Another key output from this part of the process is a clear definition of budget and resource requirements.

The second part of the calibration phase is to identify the right sources in the market to provide the requested information. In collecting this information, the technology research can sometimes be marginalized to the detriment of the quality of the output. However, in setting up the process, the firm can learn how to make this trade-off to its own satisfaction. Given that the technology threads are, at least, of short- to medium-term value to the organization, and that they will have an impact on the long-term set of products for the company, it is advisable to build a long-term source-maintenance strategy so that the information can be regularly updated and enhanced to input to the annual business strategy and technology strategy review.

Outputs from the source-identification work include a map of the source relationships (that is, how different technologies interrelate), the approach strategy to determine how to incorporate any new technology into the existing portfolio, and the maintenance strategy. In the light of the information gleaned at this stage, the technology threads can be modified or rectified, and described in more detail.

TARGET ACQUISITION

Once the technology threads are clearly defined, the firm needs to create a technology radar team consisting of resources from both R&D and other business units, and with individual roles, targets, responsibilities, budgets, and so on, specified and agreed. Outputs include a map of the roles and relationships and a communications plan for the whole of the team involved in the technology radar program. The communication process should include reports to senior management on how the process is developing and how it relates to the business strategy. At this stage, the team should be fully briefed and trained. Any tools or external resources that are required should be identified.

As the second part of this phase, the team undertakes primary market intelligence research or customer value analysis for each of the technology threads. The results include reports on meetings with external organizations, including competitors, results of patent reviews and licensing agreements, and analysis of trade shows and conference reports. The relationships between different technology sources should also be defined.

RADAR "LOCK-ON"

The final task is to convert the technology data into intelligence that can be used by all the business units involved in the process. The team will analyze all the outputs and check that any technology crossovers between technological threads and trends are identified. As with any research program, the conversion of raw market and technology information into management intelligence requires knowledge of business modelling and analysis techniques. The collection of the data will be relatively easy; the analysis and conversion of it into meaningful information that will be of business and technological benefit to the firm is a much harder set of tasks.

The result of the process includes a clear definition of the trends in the market, in terms of competitors' activities and technological developments. As a consequence, the technological implications for the firm can be defined and, in particular, how it is positioned in relation to major competitors. Those involved will now be in a position to make the necessary decisions relating to technology investment and the business performance of the company, based on a clear understanding of market and technological developments and trends.

Technology radar proved its worth for an electronics company that was interested in the market for safety and security devices in residential homes, an area in which it had no previous experience. It adopted the technology radar approach to make forecasts of the potential for technology change to have an impact on the market over the next five years and to pinpoint candidate technologies for investment. It also assessed the potential for these emerging technologies to knock out the established players and to identify any existing players who were attempting to use innovative technology to capture market share. With all the likely market and technology developments at its fingertips, it devised a market entry strategy that won the wholesale agreement of both the marketers and the technologists. It was, however, decided that although there was a good business idea to be exploited, the company did not have the right set of competencies to take it forward.

The benefits of the technology radar approach are that it is linked strongly to business unit decisions. This is possible because it can distinguish between levels of actions required, help produce better and more timely decisions, and support more effective decisions on product timing. It improves the technology base by giving early warning of threats, enabling the technology strategy input to link more effectively to longer-term product planning and aiding technology transfer and integration. Most important, it is practical, with a clear, simple, repeatable work set, and without overhead load on one individual or one department.

TECHNOLOGICAL DISCONTINUITIES IMPLY RISK, AND IT MUST BE MANAGED

Technologists can frighten managers in other parts of the firm by mentioning a single word—risk:

- "If I don't have the resources I have asked for, the risk of the project's failing increases."
- "The technology that we are employing is high-risk."
- "If marketing couldn't provide us with the information, the risks of the project's failing were bound to be high."
- "All the work we do in the R&D department has risk associated with it."

Of course, there is always risk associated with technology, but like risk in marketing, financial appraisal, and general management, it can be managed, and there are processes and techniques that enable it to be minimized.

In any R&D project, all the elements of risk must be quantified right at the beginning of the project—before one day is spent on it. The link back to the business requirements and the business risk must also be very clearly identified; otherwise, R&D may develop something that the customer does not want or that the firm is incapable of making. Note, here, the reference to the *customer*, not the marketing department.

It is not uncommon for R&D to embark on a project with very little specification of what the customer wants, especially if the project is the development of a product that is similar to one it has developed before (that is, a derivative) or is a logical next step (that is, next-generation). Even if R&D is working on a product breakout, it may well be tempted to keep its options open and so keep the initial specification as broad and unspecific as possible. It is incumbent upon both the marketing department and R&D that customer requirements be very clearly specified. Without planning and detailed specification of the project, the R&D department has absolute authority to add resource and effort without being accountable. As a result, the risk of the project's failing is bound to be high.

Where the specification is very open, or even sometimes when it is tightly defined, "creeping change" sometimes occurs, that is, frequent changes are made to the specification in development with the result that the project is prone to "run away" in terms of timescales, costs, and deliverables.* The project owner must resist all attempts at changes of specification unless the costs of the change (in terms of labor, disruption to the project, and extension of the project timescale) are repaid by a several-fold return in benefit.

There is, of course, risk involved when the firm is embarking on new technology applications or needs new core competencies. Without the right technology, however, the firm may

---

*See also Kenneth G. Cooper and Thomas Mullen (PA Consulting Group/Pugh-Roberts Associates), *"Swords and Plowshares," Guidelines for Successful Acquisition and Management of Software Intensive Systems,* U.S. Department of the Air Force, September 1994.

either produce a product that is inferior to the competition's or, worse, not deliver the project at all. Outside the R&D environment, questions should be asked about the suitability of any new technology, for on its own, R&D may well regard the need to introduce new technologies as an irresistible challenge.

Many scientists and engineers are motivated to strive for perfection. Given that the firm may be betting its future on the release of new products, it is very difficult to convince technologists that 95 percent delivery against the original budget and specification on time is better than 100 percent delivery (or worse, 110 percent delivery) three years late and twice the original budget estimate. Rigorous control, monitoring, and review processes are essential so that projects can be stopped before they get out of control and threaten the profitability of the firm.

***

The biggest risk to the chief executive, the board, and the firm's shareholders comes when products are launched late. They then have smaller windows of opportunity, with the result that increases in volume of business, in profit, and in the overall financial performance of the company are threatened. The application of techniques such as customer value analysis, technology radar, and risk analysis are all beneficial in helping to define the future product development portfolio. They also help to manage the delivery of the right products to the market at the right price and at the right time. There are few examples of firms launching a product late against the original specification and earning more revenue and profit than they originally estimated. Miracles don't happen in business.

INNOVATING TO SURVIVE

Most blue collar workers could come up with a more creative or a more efficient way of doing even the most menial tasks. Every day, every chief executive will have a myriad of creative and inventive ideas relating to his or her business. Invention and the creation of novel ideas are widespread in organizations. The difficulty is turning them into successful applications, products, or services, and it is this perceived difficulty that accounts for the failure of so many organizations to drive growth through innovation. Yet, turning ideas into deliverable products or services is a perfectly manageable process.

Innovation management is the process through which the value of *all* creative ideas is recognized, ideas are matched to market needs, and the funding, culture, and working environment are provided so that new ideas are brought to the market as quickly and as effectively as possible. This is the key to the success of many leading firms today. It is not the person who comes up with the idea so much as the one who brings the idea to fruition who should win the praise of the firm, for it is bringing the idea to fruition that drives profitable growth. The innovation process can be managed both to meet the short-term needs of the market and firm, through the incremental application of existing technical and nontechnical knowledge, and to exploit the longer-term opportunities that can be provided by the introduction of new technologies.

INNOVATION IS THE ENGINE OF GROWTH

✓ Many studies indicate the strong and positive links between companies that have formal innovation management processes in place and those that produce strong revenue growth. In 1996, the UK's most innovative companies had average annual sales growth of 7 percent; noninnovative companies turned in a rate of 5 percent. The pattern is similar in terms of export growth and growth in employment.[1] A recent study of 1000 large U.S. companies, reported in *Grow to Be Great*,[2] found the compound annual growth rate in market value of companies classified as "shrinkers" to be just 5 percent. The value of the "profitable growers" grew by 19 percent.

Companies such as Hewlett-Packard, Gillette, Johnson & Johnson, and 3M are cited as being world leaders in their respective industries, based on their ability to provide new products to meet changing market needs. A company such as Hewlett-Packard is able to derive 60 percent of its revenues from products that it has launched in the last five years. 3M derives 30 percent of its revenues from products launched in the last five years. Such performances are not achieved by luck.

Hewlett-Packard did not simply sit back when it achieved dominance of the laser-printing market. It quickly followed this success with the introduction of ink-jet technology to provide high-quality printers at affordable prices for the personal computer market and small businesses, and it continues to innovate. It appears that once the product development and innovation process starts delivering, it takes on a dynamic of its own.

---

[1]Stephen Roper et al., *Product Innovation and Development in United Kingdom, German, and Irish Manufacturing,* Northern Ireland Economic Research Centre at University of Belfast, and Fraser of Allander Institute at University of Strathclyde and ifo-Institut für Wirtschaftsforschung, March 1996.

[2]Gertz, D. L. and J. P. A. Baptista, *Grow to Be Great: Breaking the Downsizing Cycle,* The Free Press, New York, 1995.

3M has deliberately built a culture on an historical tradition of innovation. The chairman and chief executive of 3M, Livio D. DeSimone, believes that innovation is the engine of growth for 3M, and the facts support this. In 1995, 3M's operating revenues increased by $1.3 billion, two-thirds of which came from products it produced that year. A previous chairman of 3M, William MacKnight, introduced the idea that technical staff could devote 15 percent of their time to a project of their own invention. In other words, they could manage themselves for 15 percent of their time. Some technical staff do spend up to 15 percent of their time on their own projects, while others spend none at all. For 3M, it is not the amount of personal project time that is important, but the message—that there is flexibility in the business system and that the organization will tolerate employees using this time to develop new product ideas for the company.

Over time, a firm's products or services will produce diminishing returns if they are not refreshed. Once upon a time, the Singer sewing machine company and the National Cash Register (NCR) company were major multinational organizations, renowned for their products. Most of the young generation of today would not even recognize these names. The introduction of new models of sewing machines, conceived in Japan and elsewhere in Asia and based on advances in electronics, eroded Singer's markets rapidly. The early to mid-1970s saw the market ratio of electromechanical and electronic cash registers switch from 90:10 to 10:90. NCR continued to refine obsolete electromechanical technology in the face of the electronics and computer revolution. It invested in new electronic and computer-based technology too little and too late. It eventually clawed its way back to achieve some success in its industry, but what might have been?

There are, of course, also spectacular examples of firms betting the future of the business on a particular *new* product and paying dearly for getting it wrong. In the 1950s, Ford continued to invest in and eventually launched the Edsel, despite all the indications that this was not a car the market wanted. IBM continued to develop new and bigger mainframe computing systems in the 1980s in the face of the rapid introduction of personal computing and packaged software.

COMPANIES OFTEN SHY AWAY FROM INNOVATION

Growing the business through the introduction of new products and services is so compelling that it is difficult to understand why so few firms incorporate it as an integral part of their business strategy. Many complain that neither the financial institutions nor governments are keen to provide the investment necessary to promote innovation and growth. Others suggest that it is skills shortages that hinder the ability of firms to implement product-innovation processes—either the education system or training programs are letting business down. At a more local level, the arguments become more inward-focused:

- "We ought to stick to the knitting."
- "Product innovation is risky, so let's not do it."
- "Only small companies can innovate, and even they can't afford it."
- "We are in a commodity business, so there is nothing to innovate."
- "Innovators are born, and, anyway, we don't have the right resources."

For many companies, this tentativeness derives from the false association of "innovation" with "blockbuster" inventions. In fact, innovation applies to both products and processes (selling, manufacturing, delivery, service, and so on), and many forms of innovation are quite mundane. Innovation does not have to be linked to a significant technological advance. Many innovative ideas are incremental and are based on applying existing knowledge to market applications. At the basic level, it could be copying (often referred to as reverse engineering) a competitor's product. It follows that innovation is not the exclusive domain of clever scientists or technologists. It is a process that everyone can take part in.

INNOVATION NEEDS A MANAGEMENT FRAMEWORK

The most successful organizations, in whatever industry they operate, have an institutionalized process of fostering and managing innovation. Exhorting staff members from different functions to sit around a table and be creative will undoubtedly produce a raft of new ideas, but what happens to the output? Some framework for the development of innovative ideas needs to be built that can capture and evaluate *all* good ideas, both incremental and blockbuster. Market and business boundaries must be defined and a context, or focus, provided for innovation.

One useful model is illustrated in Fig. 5-1. It consists of four main stages, which, followed rigorously, force the innovation team (or teams) to focus progressively on those innovations that have the best chance of success, given the nature of the firm's business, its competencies, and the foreseen desires of its existing or potential customers.

Establishing the foundation involves the innovation team in defining the profiles of the company and the market in which it operates. *Getting the picture* requires the innovation team to define the broader market and competitive opportunities as well as assess gaps in the firm's own product portfolio. *Managing creativity* is the stage at which creative ideas are developed and progressively refined. *Planning for growth* requires a switch from idea-generation into project planning and implementation.

ESTABLISHING THE FOUNDATION

The starting point is a clear understanding that the firm has a strategy for growth, predicated on the introduction of new

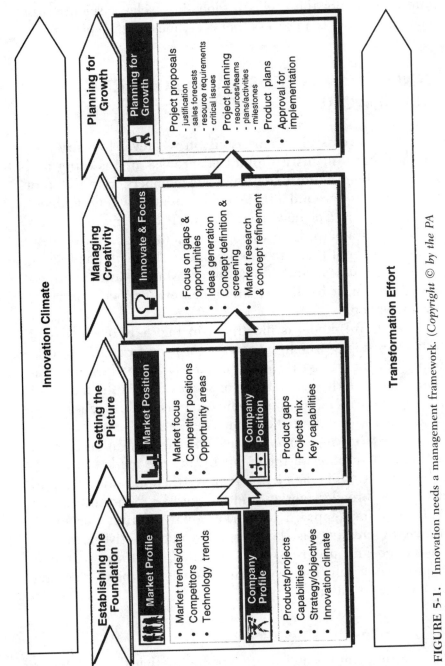

FIGURE 5-1. Innovation needs a management framework. (*Copyright © by the PA Consulting Group.*)

products or services. This strategy must be driven from the top of the firm and ingrained in the thinking of all of the business units.

No single function, be it marketing, sales, or R&D, should be alone in looking for growth opportunities. Entrepreneurial and innovative firms draw on resources throughout the firm to optimize new product opportunities. A firm's product portfolio should consist of a variety of product development projects, with each scheduled for completion to meet the market requirements of the individual product. The project should be planned to maximize the revenue and growth requirements of the firm and to make effective and efficient use of the resources in the firm.

Each project should have a nominated project manager or leader who, in turn, selects and briefs a working team, agreeing with them on the milestones and the review process to be followed throughout the project. To have the best chance of success, the team should be truly cross-functional, including active representatives from marketing, R&D, production, and so on. The availability of team members will therefore have to be negotiated with their line managers, as will responsibility for holding the project budget. A steering group, sponsored by a member from the executive ranks, should be established to oversee the outputs of the working team. This ensures that the project has good visibility throughout the firm and overt senior management support.

When an innovation team meets, its first inclination is to brainstorm to get new product ideas flowing. The experienced innovation manager, however, will resist this temptation. He or she will initiate the innovation process by undertaking a high-level profiling of the market and the firm. The market profile covers trends, sales, technology, and the market position of competitors. The firm's profile includes a review of the current portfolio, its capabilities, its technology base, and its objectives, described in the context of the marketplace. As a result, the leader and other members of the team should be able to define some initial overall goals for the project in terms of target sales, product focus, and deadlines.

GETTING THE PICTURE

The previous step can be likened to defining key pieces of a jigsaw, based on a snapshot of the market profile and the firm's profile. Major opportunities can be achieved only by evaluating a much larger and coherent picture into which the first pieces of the puzzle can fit. To do this, a more formal review of the market and the firm needs to be undertaken. This review needs to be based on relevant and up-to-date data and information.

Most firms have a plethora of data that they can access. They are often found wanting, however, in interpreting this data to provide rich and useful information. Summarizing data for the market segment of interest in a structured and coherent form can provide valuable insights into new product opportunities.

Creativity in finding good data sources can reap rewards:

- Recognizing changes in consumer behavior that will influence the future needs of consumers, for example, can provide valuable pointers for new products. In the food and drinks sector, the development of new ranges of isotonic and sports-nutritional drinks has enhanced the soft drinks market in many parts of the world.

- While some firms are reluctant to explore the capabilities of their competitors, mindful of possible retaliation, others (like Coca Cola and Pepsi Cola, or Procter & Gamble and Unilever) indulge in such fierce competition that open warfare frequently breaks out. At one extreme firms can use product tear-down to analyze competitive offerings. Alternatively, data on existing and possible future competitors can be legitimately gleaned by scanning published information relating to competitive products and being alert at conferences, where speakers usually give away a lot more than they intend.

- The technology radar process can help to highlight and summarize technology trends that could have an impact on the company or that might be exploited in the manufacture or development of new products.

- Discussions with suppliers about their technical capabilities, developments, and objectives, and with research institutes, trade associations, universities, and consultants about technology trends all help to build up a comprehensive picture of where technology is moving and what impact it might have on the firm.

The firm should already have several product development projects underway. Both current and proposed projects should be assessed against a set of criteria to rank them and identify any potential problems, such as shortages of funding or people. The criteria should be as quantitative as possible and should relate to at least three main areas: the strategic fit with the business, the market attractiveness and development timescale, and the level of innovation required. It is also a useful discipline to try to assess the expenditure that is likely to be incurred in launching the product and the incremental sales that it will deliver to the firm. An example of an evaluation process for a firm's product development program is given in Fig. 5-2.

As a rule of thumb, $1 spent on the creative process can easily translate into $10 of development effort and over $100 to launch a new product. So, in addition to undertaking a review of the development program, the team should also, in this step, assess the firm's capabilities to develop, produce, and market the new products:

- In the *R&D and technical* discipline, it must understand the strengths and weaknesses in its industry sector, where there are gaps in capabilities, what combination of critical capabilities give it a unique competence, and how any gaps can be filled.

- Its *production and operations* group must be capable of reacting quickly to changes in new product definitions, have

Current R&D Programs	Technology				Market				Strategic			
	Level of innovation	Staff skills	Critical mass	Equipment/facilities	Timescale to window (months)	New market?	Market risk (H,M,L)	Size of opportunity	Fit with BU	Type of program	New technology (Critical or enabling)	Benefit to cost
A	3	4	Y	3	6	Y	H	L	Y	D	E	H
B	2	4	N	5	18	Y	M	L	Y	N	E	H
C	5	4	Y	5	0	N	L	VL	Y	N	E	VH
D	2	3	Y	4	36	N	L	VL	N	B	C	H
E	2	3	N	4	0	N	M	L	Y	B	C	M
F	1	3	N	5	36	Y	H	L	N	N	E	M

Y = Yes
N = No
L = Large
VL = Very Large

H = High
VH = Very High
M = Medium

* Breakout (B), Next - generation (N), or Derivative (D)

Problem area - market not ready

Problem area - speed up program

Strategic problem

FIGURE 5-2. Evaluation of development programs delivers results. (*Copyright © by the PA Consulting Group.*)

excellent manufacturing processes, in-built flexibility to handle product variations, and a low (per unit) cost of production. Sourcing of raw materials, stock holding, and logistics must also be first-class.

- In *marketing*, it must understand the strengths and weaknesses of its branding strategy, how it undertakes market-driven pricing, where its advertising and promotion budget is most effectively spent, and how the effectiveness of the sales organization can be maximized.

MANAGING CREATIVITY

A good innovation manager promotes lateral thinking within the project team to search for new approaches to products and marketing. All potential sources of innovation should be reviewed and the team should be exposed to as many sources of technology and marketing ideas as possible. The product innovation team should characterize areas of opportunity in terms of trends, product, market, or technology dimensions. Gaps in the existing portfolio or opportunities to improve current performance—for example, ways of reducing warranty claims on a particular product—should be identified.

It should not be difficult to generate a long list of ideas for potential development into products and processes at this stage. Myriad suggestions usually emerge from the idea-generation phase. The difficult part is turning these diverse ideas into product concepts that the technologists can develop. Initial product concepts can often be created by clustering ideas and then filtering them according to their fit with the firm and the attractiveness of the opportunity. Various tools and techniques can be used for this, including scenario planning, strength, weakness, opportunity, threat (SWOT) analysis, and portfolio assessment. The output should be a preliminary definition of a product concept, with initial priorities, and indications of any further requirements—perhaps some consumer research or perhaps some further refinement of the concept.

The introduction of consumer and concept refinements may find little support among the technologists, who at this stage will be itching to get the product up and running. However, testing products on consumers to gauge their acceptability and to assess how they compare with a competitor's offering can be invaluable to the overall success of the project. This is all about managing risk before major investment is committed.

The output of this step will be a short list of "real" ideas, which will converge on commercial needs. These ideas for a new product can then be converted into a defined set of product goals.

PLANNING FOR GROWTH

The acid test is to break out of the idea-generation and concept stage and get the product to market. At this stage, a simple one- to two-page proposal, justifying investment to the first milestone review and highlighting the costs and major risks of the next stage of the process is adequate. The proposal must, however, contain clear descriptions of the product, its strategic fit with the business, the benefits it will bring to the firm's customers, and estimates of market size and unit costs. Preliminary financial projections and a high-level project plan should be submitted to the steering group for onward transmission to the board, if appropriate.

The project leader who has seen the project through to this stage may not be the most appropriate person to take it forward from development into production. A new project manager, or champion, with an executive sponsor on the board, may need to be nominated. Single-point responsibility must be clearly defined and communicated to the rest of the firm and the project team. There is often a good deal of uncertainty about who is truly in charge of a project. Is it the project manager or a line manager, the project sponsor, marketing, or the chief executive? Where the management of the project is ambiguous, the project stands a good chance of failure.

Key decisions need to be taken by whoever has responsibility for seeing the product through to production—timescales and budget need to agree, people and funding need to be negotiated, project review procedures and milestones need to be established, and the locations and facilities for developing the product need to be agreed.

Project monitoring and control mechanisms should be set up as part of the overall project plan, with formal tracking and review procedures to report on progress against the original plan. These mechanisms may be regarded by the R&D group as an unnecessary imposition. It is, however, imperative that disciplines applied elsewhere in the firm be applied in a similar way to the R&D organization, for without them, R&D has no accountability.

The level of management will vary according to the importance of the project and the amount of risk associated with it. If a project is defined as high-risk, at least one member of the executive or board should be involved, even if this means simply acting as chairperson of a steering committee. Positive management, however, is essential. This means that in addition to monitoring, tracking, and reviewing, active steps are taken to put the project back on course should it slip—by reallocating resources. Adherence to the formal procedures can vary from project to project. Smaller, low-risk projects, for example, should not have to bear excessive administrative overheads. For higher risk projects, particularly those consuming a lot of resources, adherence to strict, formal review procedures should be mandatory. In any event, formal reviews of *all* projects should be undertaken at regular intervals to ensure that they are delivering against the original objectives. Even small projects can eventually cause the business to hemorrhage if they continue to consume resources without delivering.

***

Innovation processes must convert creative ideas from anywhere in the firm into new products. They must therefore apply right across the firm; they are not the exclusive domain of the technologists. Leadership of the innovation process must come from the top. If the chief executive wants the company to grow, the implementation of a coherent product innovation process drawing on the skills of all key staff must be the major priority.

CASE STUDY—COCA-COLA

Innovation is the domain of everybody in the (Coca-Cola) company.

GEORGE GOURLAY

Senior Vice President and Manager,
Technical Operations Division

In the annual report for 1997 the late Roberto C. Goizueta, who had been Chairman, Board of Directors and Chief Executive Officer of The Coca-Cola Company said that the company is still unquenchably thirsty—thirsty for more ways to reach consumers, in more places, with more of its products.

In 1996 Coca-Cola produced another year of record earnings in unit sales volume. The company delivered a 43 percent return on investment and earnings per share grew by 19 percent, following a 19 percent gain in 1995. Net earnings and economic profit reached $3.5 billion and $2.7 billion respectively. At the end of 1995, Coca-Cola's market value was $93 billion; at the end of 1996 it was $131 billion. Thus $38 billion of additional share ownership wealth was created in only one year. For the second year running, Coca-Cola topped *Fortune* magazine's ranking of creators of wealth.

And yet, in Roberto Goizueta's words, "One of the world's most valuable companies, about to celebrate its 111th birthday, is only just getting started."

Roberto Goizueta often referred to many examples of companies that have forgotten the real reason why they exist, whereas in Coca-Cola the intention is to remain committed to creating value for shareholders. The way it plans to do this is by capitalizing on the virtually infinite growth opportunities that the company believes still exist for its products. Just as passionately, the company's senior managers believe that Coca-Cola must not, and will not, rest on its laurels.

It may seem incongruous that a company such as Coca-Cola should be concerned about growth and particularly the role of technology in delivering it, but George Gourlay, Senior Vice President and Manager of the Technical Operations

Division, talks at length about the company's mission to "create value for our shareowners on a long term basis."

George considers that Coca-Cola is not a high-technology organization but a marketing company. Everything that it does is driven by meeting the needs of its consumers, and to this end the roles of technology, engineering, and R&D are extremely important.

To begin with, before launching new products or delivering extensions of current products, a great deal of research is undertaken. This is not just in terms of basic market research but in clearly understanding what motivates the consumer.

The engineering department also has a major role to play in assisting with the packaging and engineering of the products. In particular, the department is responsible for looking five to ten years ahead into technologies that may be of interest to Coca-Cola. For example, in bottling this will mean the evaluation of new plastics to improve production processes and address environmental issues.

Equally, the application of innovative technologies is an ongoing process in developing new packaging media for Coca-Cola's products. This is particularly important given the brand name of Coca-Cola and the image associated with the famous Coca-Cola bottle. During 1997 the company began test marketing a new 12-ounce contour can inspired by the original Coca-Cola bottle, packaging which utilizes the latest can shaping technology and is designed to instantly differentiate Coca-Cola from straight-walled soft drink cans in the marketplace. The new two-piece aluminum can has been in development for several years using a combination of the company's expertise and that of its suppliers, a packaging breakthrough which is part of the continuing effort by the company to both enhance and further differentiate its products through proprietary packaging.

George Gourlay's view is that the people who work for Coca-Cola develop their products, and it is important, to be effective in the market, that the company harness the skills of all groups of expertise. The engineers must harness the technology, marketing must provide the consumer insights, production must produce the goods, and all the various groups must work together for the good of shareowners.

Equally, senior management believes that it is vital for the health of the organization to have continued organic growth and for Coca-Cola to grow existing markets. It must, however, differentiate itself by adopting new technologies as and when it can, and under no circumstances can Coca-Cola afford to be complacent about its success in the marketplace.

In terms of R&D activities within the company, Coca-Cola invests very little of its own resources in basic research. It believes it is important to understand the fundamentals of its products, processes, and packaging technologies, but what is more important is to know where to go to get research and development expertise which the company can harness. In George's estimation if a company does basic research in-house, it tends to have problems looking for solutions for the outputs of the research. For Coca-Cola, intelligent utilization of existing and evolving technology is the name of the game.

The approach to the exploitation of development is very focused. Coca-Cola taps into institutions that are at the leading edge of technology, preferring to access the developments of other institutions and other suppliers. However, it is critical that technical people have the skills to present complicated technologies in ways that senior managers can understand and can evaluate in terms of the value-added that such technologies will bring to the company.

Value-based management is used throughout Coca-Cola to understand how to create and add value. It is a strongly held belief that cost reduction for its own sake can destroy value. For example, the development of the plastic contoured bottle added cost in the production process. However, its introduction drove volume, increased market share, added value to the consumers, and created value for the shareowners of the Coca-Cola Company.

Using conventional economic thinking in terms of the packaging process at least, this new packaging development should not have seen the light of day.

Within Coca-Cola every R&D and engineering product is

included in the business plan in terms of how it is going to grow the business, add value, and support the marketing drive. Given the company's ambitious and aggressive growth targets, the key in Coca-Cola is not the amount of capital and financial investments the company has to make but the necessary investment in people. In effect, Gourlay believes that too much skill development is based on existing, or historic, needs as opposed to developing the skills and competencies now, that will be needed in the future.

A future role of the technology group is to change the mindsets of the people involved in development opportunities and by doing so help to change the culture of the company. Part of this process is to get the marketing and development departments to "think outside their boxes." George Gourlay says, "Innovation is the domain of everybody in the company, and everyone who works for Coca-Cola is encouraged never to be satisfied with what they have currently achieved but to think more about what they still have to do in the future."

For R&D, thinking out of the box is done by encouraging the group to apply knowledge gained from suppliers, the Coca-Cola engineering capabilities, other industries, and academia. As part of this process for sharing knowledge, the company has instituted the position of Chief Learning Officer, whose role it is to develop systems to facilitate collaboration among the various internal groups in the most effective way. This collaboration is based on leveraging knowledge and developing means of building partnerships and alliances with other organizations whereby Coca-Cola is able to exploit innovation processes. An important aspect of the success of the company's innovation process is that assessment of costs is always important but not decisive.

Coca-Cola also encourages suppliers to work with them, using the company's core competency in understanding the consumer so that jointly they can meet the consumer's needs. This is because the company is adamant that it will not be a commodity supplier, believing that if it works with its suppliers to differentiate its products, processes, and packaging, it will continue to provide products that consumers really want.

George Gourlay is convinced that the development-to-launch time for new products and packaging should be as short as possible, and efforts are currently being made to reduce this period. "However, this brings with it a higher level of risk—real or perceived."

In many organizations, risk aversion is something that individuals are quite happy to engage in. However, risk aversion at both the individual and company level can destroy value. The process that senior management is trying to instill at Coca-Cola is therefore to take intelligent risks, which requires a major effort in developing a strong culture of innovation throughout the company but in a structured way.

As far as the future is concerned, Gourlay believes that there is a great deal of opportunity and excitement for Coca-Cola and its consumers. In addition, developments in distributions systems will enable the company to manufacture and distribute its products to the marketplace more effectively and efficiently.

The development of Coca-Cola's staff is also a key factor for the future. This development will include improving their business skills, undertaking more value-based analysis of their work, application of risk management techniques, and protecting Coca-Cola's position through the judicious use of intellectual property rights and patents.

The move from being a functionally based business to one that implements more effective business processes across units to meet the needs of its customers is a transition that is making a difference. George Gourlay is clear that future developments of the business have, therefore, to be driven by consumers and their anticipated needs in the future. "In this respect," says Gourlay, "everything that Coca-Cola's Engineering Development undertakes is more than simply development, but is fundamental to the company's future success."

MANAGING THE DELIVERY PROCESS

As technologies proliferate, products become multitechnology-based, customers become more demanding, and the pressure on organizations to show a faster and very positive return on investment in technology grows, it is unlikely that any firm, no matter how big, will be able to survive on its own R&D resources. The response is likely to be a growing trend toward outsourcing, the advent of the "virtual" R&D organization, or the setting up of collaborative agreements between firms. The choice of a particular option will depend on the culture of the company, the confidence of the R&D organization, its propensity to accept change, the priorities of senior management, and the nature of the technologies that the company needs to develop.

Well planned and managed, these options will provide the more entrepreneurial firms with a wider technology base to support national and international growth. They are not, however, without their pitfalls.

KEEPING ALL R&D WORK IN-HOUSE IS LIKELY TO ISOLATE AND LIMIT THE FIRM

For many companies, the idea of having *any* R&D work undertaken by a third party is not to be contemplated. They are probably the companies that have a very strong technological base and a head of technology who believes the firm's technological capability is so strategically important that she or he could not entertain the use of external resources. If that R&D organization manages itself so superbly, recruits so successfully, and monitors worldwide developments so perceptively that it genuinely has no need to buy in any expertise, it should be showing a return on growth and an increase in shareholder value, year after year, that far outstrips the performance of any other firm in its sector or, indeed, of any other firm in any sector. Alternatively, it will find itself, sometimes very quickly, totally isolated from developments in the market, producing product derivatives, and meeting customer service requirements that will become significant overheads to the business and make no contribution to the firm's growth.

WISE OUTSOURCING OF PRODUCT DEVELOPMENT CAN LEAD TO TECHNOLOGY LEADERSHIP

There is a common trend in Europe, the United States, and Japan for companies to rely more and more on external resources for R&D activities. According to various studies, European companies spend between zero and 10 percent of their total R&D budgets *outside* the company. In the United Kingdom, the figure is around 16 percent. This is a trend that is growing quite dramatically around the world, as Fig. 6-1

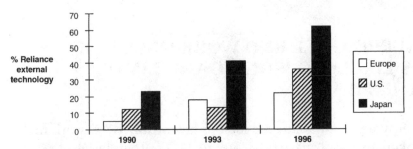

FIGURE 6-1.   Industrial R&D outsourcing is increasing dramatically. (*Copyright © 1993, PA/MIT Global Benchmarking Study.*)

illustrates. In theory, this increase in outsourcing should move firms into the upper reaches of the technology leadership league. Unfortunately, it doesn't. Many firms are failing to see the pitfalls inherent in the complex business of outsourcing in this area. These fall into three main categories: giving in to the temptation to outsource research rather than development, failing to be rigorous about what is sensible and profitable to outsource, and failing to take account of the very different demands that will be made on management when large proportions of the firm's development budget are going to a third party.

RESIST THE TEMPTATION TO OUTSOURCE RESEARCH

Much of the outsourcing quoted above is research activity, rather than development or product breakout, as Fig. 6-2 illustrates.

However, as outsourced research does not contribute to technology leadership, the beneficiaries of this activity are the traditional centers of research excellence, including academic institutions and contract R&D organizations, rather than the firms that are funding it (see Fig. 6-3). As we discussed in Chapter 2, funding research projects is simply supporting institutional curiosity in the hope that the gamble might pay off. Interestingly, it is firms in buoyant and growing sectors, like pharmaceuticals and telecommunications, that are much

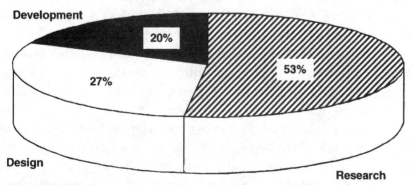

FIGURE 6-2.   Research rather than development is commonly outsourced. (*Copyright © 1994, PA Consulting Group Survey of UK Industry.*)

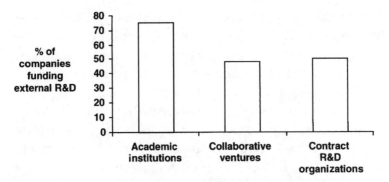

FIGURE 6-3. The beneficiaries of outsourced research are the traditional centers of research excellence. (*Copyright © 1994, PA Consulting Group Survey of UK Industry.*)

more likely to be outsourcing development activity; the UK engineering industry, currently in a poor state, outsources a lot of low-level research and very little new product development and innovation.

The technology leaders will be those that outsource product development and product breakout in a structured and timely way. Proactively seeking and managing technology outside their own company will enable them to exploit technology faster and more cheaply than their competitors.

BE RIGOROUS ABOUT DECIDING WHAT TO OUTSOURCE

The tale of the dodo is well known. This was a bird that was indigenous to Mauritius. Over a period of several hundred years, it had become very secure in its habitat and no longer saw any need to fly. In the sixteenth century, the island became a popular stopping off point for pirates—indeed, hungry pirates. The bird itself was particularly ugly but the meat was both enjoyable and easy to obtain. As a result, the dodo quickly became extinct. A management consultant's advice to the dodo would have been to have kept up its core competency, that is, its ability to fly, and, more important, not to become overconfident and complacent or someone will eat you. Today, there are still a lot of pirates out there.

As technology becomes more complex and the need for innovation increases, the danger for the R&D organization is in becoming complacent, shifting away from its core competency and/or ignoring what is going on in the rest of the world. R&D organizations are often too close to the technological issues and cannot see the wider market and business developments.

The starting point for the outsourcing process must always be the business strategy and the technology strategy that supports it. Then, it will be clear what the development priorities are, and whether the firm has, in-house, the competencies to deliver them in the required timescale.

The original work by Hamel and Prahalad on core competencies was encapsulated in their award-winning 1990 article in the *Harvard Business Review*.[1] The concept of core competencies is that they are specialized areas of expertise, which usually result from the coordination or integration of diverse skills. Core competency analysis provides a means of reviewing where a business's strengths and weaknesses lie and how these can be consolidated to provide it with distinct advantages over its competition.

Alternatively, gaps in competency can be assessed so that these can be filled either by recruitment, outsourcing, or acquisition of the missing skills. The process of identifying and determining core competencies is based on conducting a review of the business activities and building up a hierarchy of primary capabilities and critical capabilities all of which, when consolidated at the highest level, define the particular areas of competency or competitive advantage (Fig. 6-4).

At the lowest level, primary capabilities enable a business to undertake its normal nondifferentiated business activities and operations. These capabilities are typically functional, technical, or business processes and provide no discernible advantage in the market. Critical capabilities are the next level in the hierarchy and consist of functions, skills, and business processes that can have a direct impact on the competitive

---

[1]G. Hamel and C. K. Prahalad, "The Core Competencies of the Corporation," *Harvard Business Review*, May-June 1990, pp. 79–91.

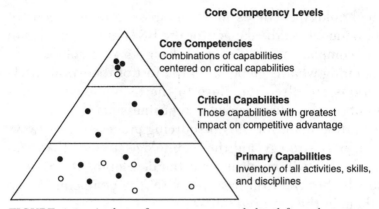

FIGURE 6-4. Analysis of core competency helps define what can or needs to be outsourced. (*Copyright © 1997 by the PA Consulting Group.*)

position of the business. They include capabilities such as technology know-how or science, a person with a specific set of skills, or a key business process.

A core competency exists when one, or a cluster of critical capabilities and primary capabilities in combination, provides the company with real, sustainable business advantage. In particular, a core competency will have several distinct qualities:

- It provides significant competitive advantage.
- It can be translated into customer-perceived value.
- It is sustainable.
- It is ideally extendable to new markets.
- It is difficult to imitate.

It is possible to group core competencies into three types. A set of core *market interface* competencies provides a firm with the ability to access, serve, and shape markets uniquely well. A core *infrastructure* competency enables a firm to have the ability to manage internal operations efficiently and effectively. With both of these competencies, companies are tending to converge toward similar targets in terms of their competitive capabilities, thereby reducing the differentiation between firms. Core *technical* competencies, on the other hand, provide a firm with the ability to bring into being products and services with unique attributes that customers value. As a result, technical competencies can be the most significant source of competitive differentiation.

The highest-priority development projects should be those that are critical to driving up shareholder value. It is probable, but not always the case, that those are the projects for which the firm has the core competencies available in-house.

A firm will be less sensitive about outsourcing projects concerned with the development of derivatives of existing product ranges or with the development of service management offerings. These types of projects usually involve "enabling technologies," which offer limited market differentiation. The firm does not risk losing any competitive edge by outsourcing them to a third party because it can retain its intellectual property rights and manage the contractor effectively. The firm can then focus its own internal R&D efforts on those projects that have greatest impact on increasing revenue and shareholder value and on building additional core competencies to stay at the leading edge of technology in its sector.

There will be cases where a firm has no option but to outsource the development of critical technologies—for instance, where many technologies are involved in the development of a project or where complex software, which the original R&D organization does not have the skills to develop, is being introduced into a product range. There are risks, however: in the potential loss of intellectual property rights to the development, in the loss of competitive advantage, and in the exposure of key technological knowledge outside the firm's own sphere of control.

The key to the successful management of this option is to ensure that the project definition, the financial and market implications, and the overall objectives of the process are clearly articulated within the firm and that management controls are put in place to ensure that the critical technologies are delivered just as if the development were being undertaken internally.

Recognize that Outsourcing Requires a Different Management Style and Skills

Successfully managing an outsourced activity requires very different mindsets and skills from managing an in-house R&D department. Critical to doing it well is achieving a careful balance of advantage for the two parties involved; the outcome should be a win/win for both the firm and the contractor.

In support of this, a recent study by PA Consulting Group[2] identified great variations in the degree of success of outsourcing contracts. The most important contributors to the successful outsourcing of contracts were:

- The outsourcing activity was well defined.
- Roles and responsibilities of all parties were clear.
- There was a good relationship with the supplier.
- There was a high quality of service from the supplier.
- There was effective management of the client relationship and continuous monitoring of the outsourcing service.

The survey showed that the choice of supplier and the foundations laid during the selection process for the subsequent working relationship are key factors in setting up effective outsourcing contracts. The increased complexity of outsourcing demands more sophisticated management, particularly where the outsourcing is in a complex area and, perhaps, on a global scale. Contracts can, themselves, become very complex, so management needs to be familiar with contract types and pricing mechanisms to avoid misunderstandings.

Many firms recognize that outsourcing decisions must be taken at a strategic rather than a technical level, and they may be prepared to act strategically. They also have to commit

---

[2]PA Consulting Group, *Strategic Sourcing: International Survey*, London, 1996.

their own time and attention to it, however, to make it work successfully.

THE VIRTUAL R&D ORGANIZATION HAS A CULTURE OF NETWORKING WITH THE MOST APPROPRIATE RESOURCES

"Virtual R&D" is not just another name for outsourcing. The philosophy of the virtual R&D organization is that within the firm, technology is managed by the creative application of new technologies and the configuration of existing technologies within the firm to generate maximum business advantage. The virtual R&D organization strives to achieve this by accessing the most "business-relevant" technology from the most competent sources. These sources need not be in-house. In fact, a virtual R&D organization will probably obtain more technology inputs and developments from external sources than from in-house resources.

It will develop and install its own processes for finding and integrating external technologies, similar to the "technology radar" concept, so that it has comprehensive access to the best technologies in any part of its sector, in related sectors, and in any part of the world. Given that these external sources are a critical component of the virtual R&D organization, it must be set up so that it can use the most appropriate and effective collaborative arrangements to give it access to critical and emerging technologies. It will operate on a variable rather than a fixed-cost basis and will manage development and innovation processes against such a complex, but stable, funding and financial regime. It therefore behaves quite differently from the traditional R&D group.

One of the main differentiators of the virtual R&D organization is that it creates a culture of networking with the most appropriate resources, and it consistently delivers excellence in next-generation products and product breakouts on time and within budget and specification. In the most extreme case, it can mean that the firm relies on a global network of external organizations, which can be activated on a project-by-project basis. It is particularly suitable for the rapid development of emerging technologies, because it relies on a highly flexible, responsible, and innovative R&D "team," it has virtually no R&D opportunity costs, and it has a clear set of management and control mechanisms against which the project(s) have to deliver.

The automotive industry is likely to be one of the first in which the virtual R&D organization becomes well established. Year after year, the complexity of automobiles increases. In addition to developments in engine technology, materials technology, and traction control, creative developments are occurring in myriad allied areas, such as complex sensor technology for crash and impact protection, optoelectronics and optical fibre developments for communicating with and controlling all of the electrical systems within the car, guidance and positioning technology, active safety devices, emission control to reduce pollution, battery technology, drive by wire, and in-car communications and entertainment systems.

Given the vagaries of the market, no automotive manufacturer can afford to set up, manage, and finance an effective R&D department of such scope, probably dispersed in several technology centers around the world, and remain a viable organization that continues to grow in volume and profit. All of them will buy components from thousands of suppliers and put them together, in designs and ranges developed by their own R&D organizations, to produce a range of products that customers want, at a price they can afford.

GOOD COLLABORATION CAN BE A SOURCE OF REVENUE OR OF NEW TECHNOLOGY

We have seen that, given the pressure on firms to improve their financial performance, few of them can profitably continue to "go it alone" in the area of technological development and innovation. Yet these same pressures make the very idea of industrial collaboration with a potential competitor complete anathema to many. However, by collaborating both with competitors and cooperating firms, with management systems in place to guarantee control over the outcome, firms can derive enormous mutual benefit. The nature of such collaboration depends upon what the parties to the arrangement want to achieve. There is a spectrum of options, ranging from simple licensing of technology or the implementation of a technology agreement to full-scale mergers and acquisitions.

Make Licensing Agreements to Create Revenue or Speed Up the Development Process

Licensing agreements work in two ways. A firm may license another company in another part of the world to have access to its technology (including complete products) such that additional revenues accrue to the firm. Alternatively, if a firm needs a particular technology in support of its business strategy but cannot or does not wish to develop all of it in-house, it may enter into a technical agreement to import that technology. In high-technology sectors, like information technology, biotechnology, and new materials, the number of such agreements has increased markedly over the last few years. Between information technology companies, for instance, the number of technical agreements, whereby technical information was exchanged to speed up the outcomes of development projects, doubled between 1984 and 1989, as Table 6-1 shows. Particularly active were Siemens, Olivetti, and Philips.

The technical agreement is probably the easiest form of collaboration to set up. It requires no new company to be established and probably very little, if any, restructuring within the firms making the agreement. What it does require is a very clear definition of the scope of the collaboration—the contributions and the outputs required from the agreement by the participating firms. In general, because they are so tightly defined and specified, technical agreements are more likely to result in

Table 6-1. In the 1980s, There Was a
Twofold Growth in Agreements Between IT
Corporations

Company	1980–84	1985–89
Motorola	53	68
Siemens	51	134
IBM	48	108
Fujitsu	46	78
Olivetti	42	110
Philips	40	127
Total	280	625

SOURCE: Organization for Economic Cooperation and Development,
Technology and the Economy: The Key Relationships, Paris, 1992.
(Adapted from Table 53. Reproduced by permission of the OECD.)

technology transfer than the launch of a new product onto the
market. They therefore tend to be used to speed up the development process and to fill gaps in technical competency.

USE DEVELOPMENT PARTNERSHIPS TO POOL R&D CAPABILITY

In a development partnership, organizations pool R&D capability in the hope that the best of both will lead to the development of new, leading-edge, and innovative products. Given that
the firms involved tend to have their own objectives and agendas for the collaboration and, probably, their own undisclosed
business intentions, most such collaborations end up providing
a technological solution to a problem rather than a specific
new product. On occasions, they can lead to a merger or to the
acquisition of one firm by another. The development partnership is often predicated on combining technical skills or competencies from two complementary businesses. However, care
needs to be taken that one firm in the alliance is not learning
or gaining more than the other(s). This tends to happen where
one firm has its hidden agenda and is more focused and quick-
er at learning than its partner. Alliances usually last only a matter of years, and when they break up, one of the parties always
seems to emerge the stronger from the collaboration.

Enter into Joint Ventures to Develop New Streams of Business

A much more formal process, which requires setting up a separate company, is the joint venture. The involvement of equity in the venture can be beneficial, since it implies a degree of stability or permanence. The objective here is to target new streams of business on the basis of new products and services to be launched on the market, which could not be achieved by one company alone. For example, a firm may not have the financial resources to fund new product development from start to finish. Alternatively, it may recognize a potential market opportunity that can be seized by combining complementary technical skills.

The joint venture is set up as a separate legal entity, and the decision to transfer key R&D resources is not to be undertaken lightly. For any firm to take this step—that is, the transfer of key R&D resources—it needs to be confident that any new jointly developed technology will manifest itself quickly in revenue and profit generation. Timescales for growth in projects may be measured in months rather than in years. Depending on their various capabilities, the firms involved may provide funds, resources, or infrastructure. The participating firms will expect the joint venture to generate revenues and, very important, profit. The profit will be shared according to the amount of investment provided by each firm. This, however, can be one of the major pitfalls of a joint venture. Unrealistic targets for generating revenues and profits, particularly when the joint venture company is in its infancy, can lead to its demise.

Create Mergers or Make Acquisitions to Acquire a Technology Base or Entrepreneurial Skills

The technology base of the firm can also be extended by merging with or acquiring another company. The successful merger of two large firms to combine technology capability is extremely difficult and high-risk. In the late 1980s, for example, many telecommunications companies considered it strategically essential to acquire a computing company (or vice versa) to exploit the synergies of the integration of communications networks and developing computing systems. AT&T acquired NCR for $7.5 billion in 1991. The subsequent restructuring of AT&T indicates that the acquisition was much more difficult than expected.

More common is the acquisition of a small company by a larger firm to take on board its technological base and entrepreneurial skills. Critical here is to be sensitive to the likely cultural differences between the two organizations. If the cultural issues are not handled carefully, those with the entrepreneurial skills will very quickly move to or set up other small entrepreneurial companies. Many companies believe that growth is easiest to achieve through the mergers and acquisitions route. However, many companies base their business strategy of merging with or acquiring companies on the basis of buying customers or market share.

Just as compelling is merging or acquiring another firm on the basis of capturing technology-based skills and competencies that may take too long to develop in-house. Acquiring technology competencies is a valid method of creating value, but it should be done with caution.

Buying technology skills and competencies means that the firm must be more than adept at integrating skills into the firm. In particular, it must know what it can do with them in the future and not rely too heavily on what has happened in the past.

Some key industries are changing rapidly, based on technological change brought about by the market and the key players in the industry. For example, financial services and software are two industries that provide a significant amount of product "churn." With product life cycles sometimes measured in months rather than years, building up skills or competencies organically to compete in these markets (since the development of skills internally can take years) is not an option. Acquisition in this case is therefore a compelling option.

Given that one firm may be compelled to acquire another, however, what does this say about the buyer? For one thing, if the purchasing firm was not able to manage its own technology skills, what makes it believe that it can manage a combined set of skills? The combination of two R&D organizations is not simply a doubling of complexity but, more probably, an order of magnitude more difficult. It is, however, an unfortunate fact of business life that many acquisitions are value-destroying rather than value-creating. One key reason must be the inability of firms to exploit the combined strengths of the new technology base.

***

There are many routes to leveraging greater outputs from R&D and managing the delivery process. They range from intelligent outsourcing to acquiring new skills or a better technology base. Whatever the route, the chief executive must be deeply involved in the process to ensure that any financial investment that is made shows the best possible returns.

CASE STUDY—REUTERS

Even closer working between marketing and development is needed as we move into the 21st Century.

MARTIN DAVIDS
Director, Staff Development and Efficiency Program

Reuters is an information company. Established in the 1850s when Paul Julius Reuter used pigeons to carry share prices between Brussels and Aachen, the company now has offices in 91 countries and 217 cities around the world.

Electronically delivered financial information services for the world's business community account for more than 90 percent of Reuters' turnover, as foreign exchange dealers in Tokyo, commodity traders in Chicago, stockbrokers in London, and bankers in Switzerland subscribe to products which include real-time financial data, transaction systems, access to numerical and text or historical databases, news, graphics, still photos, and news video.

Reuters provides data feeds to financial markets and software tools to enable financiers to analyze data on currencies, stocks, futures, options, and other instruments. The company's transaction products enable traders to deal from their keyboards in foreign exchange, futures, options, and securities. As a result, Reuters' services are in demand by financial and other institutions, and its success is driven critically by the speed, accuracy, and quality of information supplied.

In the last 20 years Reuters has undergone phenomenal growth in business, both in revenue and profit, and is now widely regarded as a leading information services provider to the world business community.

In the 1970s the R&D department of Reuters designed and built operating systems, network protocols, and even PCs for its information systems services, becoming very adept at building features into its computing systems and the vast national and international network that was provided to support financial services transactions.

Part of the reason for doing this was that the necessary technology was not readily available to provide the required speed and reliability. However, in undertaking its own developments, it found that the path to getting the IT industry to meet some of its and the market's requirements was not always smooth—for example, when it wanted to implement sophisticated, change-tolerant database technology. In the latter case, as a compromise, Reuters developed a system within central research which, although not perfect, was able to meet the requirements of the time.

According to Martin Davids, significant increases in the number and quality of suppliers of information technology products and services, including organizations such as Microsoft, convinced Reuters to slowly reduce undertaking R&D on its own behalf in preference to exploiting offerings from the broader IT industry. As a result, Reuters closed its in-house manufacturing capability for terminals and other networking devices and concentrated on adding value to developments in the broader software and hardware communications and information services industry. The strength of Reuters has been to reduce its own research and development efforts as suitable "off-the-shelf" alternatives emerge.

This route was not risk-free or without problems. Indeed, Reuters had a number of difficulties when trying to adapt some new technologies in its products. However, the company persevered with buying-in other technologies and became convinced that the strength of its development today is in spotting technological changes as they occur in the industry and then adapting them for its own use. This has happened in both the computing and communications technology it applies to its products and services and in tracking the changes driven by its partners in technology.

Using as much off-the-shelf technology as possible to develop its information services enables Reuters to spend more effort on the quality and breadth of the information content provided to its customers. It also uses state-of-the-art technology from telecommunications carriers or operators to deliver information to its customers. In this respect, a major change has been the incorporation of software designed for the World Wide Web to integrate services and present them in a single, user-friendly format. Analysts now have access to research reports from brokers around the world. They are able to display this beside live information on how shares are performing. The new system includes a database of historic information and integrated into the total package is the Reuters Financial Television Service.

Martin Davids' concern is to ensure that the culture within Reuters continues to assess what is happening in the technology market that the company can exploit. For example, it reviewed the market for database search engines as part of its enhancement of current services. The future, according to Davids, is that Reuters will articulate a product or market problem or opportunity and then assess which technologies and partners can help in the development process. Where possible, it will try to exploit de facto or industry rather than proprietary or supplier-specific standards. However, it is often surprised at how little common and agreed standardization there is even today in the IT industry.

Given the volatility of the IT market, Davids sees the need for collaboration and outsourcing as being an important factor in the development of new products and services. Where Reuters is outsourcing, for example with databases, it has recognized the need for producing "invitations to tender" which it can then evaluate within a very formal and structured process.

Choosing technology partners for Reuters to work with is much more complex. To begin with, Davids believes that the partner has to be chosen for logical and rational reasons. His experience shows partner relationships follow a particular pattern. Initially, recognizing that Reuters is a demanding customer, the supplier does everything possible to show willingness, flexibility, and determination to make the partnership work. In time, the relationship and partnership come under great pressure, to the extent that Reuters has to start fighting to get attention from the supplier, while at the same time, the supplier is learning more and more about Reuters' business and translating this into opportunities in its own market.

However, some development partnerships have been very successful. For example, the Reuters/Intel partnership has been running since the late 1980s, and Reuters believes its development requirements and ability to exploit chips provided by Intel has benefited its business. In turn, Intel ensures that Davids feels he is a valued customer, even to the extent of asking him to contribute to the annual appraisal of the Intel account manager for Reuters!

For the future, Davids recognizes that Reuters cannot be complacent in having converted itself from its original roots as a news agency into one of the world's leading electronic publishing and information services providers. Reuters will have to work hard to maintain this position by building on its competencies, with its development processes for the future being built on four factors.

To begin with, Reuters has to continue to provide a cost-effective architecture for the distribution of its services. This means more connectivity and more services being provided to the market. Because product and service delivery is getting cheaper, it is extremely important for Reuters to develop services and products which keep on the right side of the cost curve, with each component of the services having to be continually reevaluated to ensure they are developed, provided, and maintained at optimal cost. In other words, the challenge is to optimize the use of commoditized components and maximize the opportunities for specific added value.

Second, the journalistic roots of Reuters have led, over the years, to a culture of getting products and services out and into the market as quickly as possible. However, this can conflict with the need to provide high quality and reliable services. The balancing of time-to-market pressures with the need to maintain quality has been handled well by Reuters. However, in the future, time-to-market for new products and services will prove more of a problem because technologies and technological solutions available off the shelf from competitors will pose a significant threat.

In Martin Davids' estimation there is still room for improvement in time-to-market, and measures have to be provided to ensure that product and service launches are of the highest quality.

Third, Davids believes that the development process itself is getting better. The increased use of external technologies is generating more ideas for new products and services. Bottom line productivity and efficiency are increasing with the applications of new tools and diagnostics. One area being given particular attention is that the development processes need to be managed more rigorously. All too often, quality can suffer at the expense of speeding up development processes, resulting in the necessity of reworking the software development applications.

However, development of IT products and services is now being judged in many IT companies against "Internet Time," whereby defensive product development and project management is being replaced by offensive product development and project management. This means there is a greater need for concurrent engineering and better management of risk to improve time to market by up to a factor of seven!

The final factor relates to staff. In the past Reuters used a functional organizational model wherein individual staff groups were placed in their boxes of development, operations, help desk, and so on, the classical model used by many organizations. A number of years ago Reuters instigated a program in which the focus switched to projects, predicated on ensuring that each project has defined and achievable business benefits to deliver.

Teams are formed and closed down by project according to the demand of each business requirement. The programs are overlaid across functions and address the local and global development issues. This requires a great deal of personal interaction by senior managers and project leaders because the local and global issues can cause self-inflicted problems if they are not managed correctly. Given that Reuters has also had to integrate a number of companies it has acquired, this has led to what Davids calls "acquisition digestion."

The substantial increase in Reuters' business, demonstrated by the 17 percent rise in profits to £701 million reported for the financial year ending December 31, 1996, has been achieved through very hard work within the organization, particularly by staff associated with service development. In the future this is not going to get any easier. The fivefold increase in the use of Reuters' network over the last two years is going to be seen as a benchmark both by the company's shareholders and its customers.

The challenge for Reuters in achieving continued growth is to make sure that the development functions deliver what the technologists believe they can deliver and what the company's marketers believe the market wants. And if Reuters is going to continue to grow from success to success, even closer working is going to be required from these two groups as the premier international news and financial information agency moves into the 21st century.

MANAGING CREATIVITY TO DELIVER TECHNOLOGY LEADERSHIP

Within every organization, various functional groups are categorized according to the culture of the company. Corporate staff in some organizations, for example, are regarded as "seagulls" that fly into a business unit, make a mess, and then fly out again. Corporate staff in other firms may genuinely live up to their claim that they are there to help. Some marketers are classified as overpaid executives with open-ended expense accounts who deliver very little added value to the firm but milk the successes and duck the failures of new product initiatives. Others are highly regarded for the value they add, based on their knowledge of the industry, of developments in the market, and of the firm's customers.

One group, however, often stands apart from the rest of the organization, whose perceptions of it are notably consistent. This is the R&D organization. R&D is full of highly educated people. Most are passionate about the discipline in which they operate, and for many, this passion leads to very focused and sometimes introverted perceptions of what the firm needs to do and where it should be going.

The culture that is thus created in the R&D organization at times sits uncomfortably with the rest of the business. The

107

problem is often compounded because R&D is usually also structurally isolated from the rest of the organization. However, if senior management is to deliver growth and increase shareholder value from technology, it has to come to grips with the whole question of R&D's relationship with the rest of the firm. Its culture is one aspect of this. The organizational integration of R&D is the other.

R&D'S CULTURAL RESISTANCE TO CHANGE MUST NOT BE ALLOWED TO HOLD SWAY

Given that the R&D organization should be and is coming under mounting pressure to become more effective and efficient, change programs are going to have to be implemented, and as with any change process, some parts will be accepted by the organization and others will be rejected. The acceptance, rejection, and ultimate acceptability of any change process depend on the cultural style of the firm as a whole, but particularly on the culture developed and nurtured within the R&D organization.

The traditional R&D organization is culturally quite resistant to change. First, with most scientists and technologists, it is the personal/professional agenda that takes precedence over corporate aspirations, which will therefore tend to be resisted if they happen not to coincide. Second, the scientific fascination with detail means that technologists require analysis and study of why change is necessary and become much more change-resistant than others.

The argument that R&D is different and should therefore be immune to change is not, however, one that senior managers should countenance. They must, on the contrary, ensure that the cultural barriers are broken down so that they provide no hindrance to the firm's efforts to drive growth through the better management of R&D.

A FIRM'S CULTURE AFFECTS ITS ABILITY TO CHANGE

Most people understand the word "culture," but very few can define what it really means in a business context. The problem with culture in the business environment is that it manifests itself on many different levels. At the highest level, a national culture will distinguish English from French, Americans from Europeans, and so on. Excluding other cultural distinctions based on language, regions, and cities, we come to the level of corporate culture, in other words, the way in which attitudes are expressed within a firm. At the next level is the culture of a particular function within the firm, like sales, marketing, manufacturing, and R&D. Further down, there are often cultural distinctions within subsections of particular functions, like the different behaviors and motivations of chemists and process engineers within an R&D organization, for example. Differences can also be noticed even between geographically dispersed groups of chemists within an organization. These small groups are often described as "subcultures" and can demonstrate wide variances from the values and behaviors observed at higher levels.

The problem with cultural differences in an organization is that they lead to different attitudes, agendas, perceptions, and influences. These, in turn, dictate differences in attitudes toward authority, bureaucracy, creativity, accountability, interrelationships, and priorities. Although different cultures may use the same words, cultural biases tend to cloud perceptions of how particular suggestions or directives will be perceived in other cultures. As a result, it becomes difficult to implement change, gives rise to conflict where there should be collaboration, creates misunderstanding, and suboptimizes effective and efficient working throughout the organization.

TRADITIONAL R&D CULTURES MAKE R&D RESISTANT TO CHANGE

R&D organizations very often have their own sets of values and behaviors that define a particular R&D "culture." On a superficial level, this manifests itself in a distinctive dress mode and a propensity to communicate in what others describe as "technospeak." On a more profound level, however, two distinguishing features of the R&D culture have the potential to slow down or even scotch attempts to bring about significant change in corporate goals, policies, products, and services. These are the technologists' primary interest in their own pursuit of knowledge, and their predilection for detail rather than the grand picture.

THE PERSONAL AGENDA VERSUS THE BUSINESS'S NEEDS

Given that any change program must be driven from the top, it should be recognized that senior scientists and technologists prize highly their standing and status with external bodies, professional institutes, and their peers. Having spent a large part of their careers striving for such recognition, they may regard changes driven by the business needs of the firm as less important than their own individual agendas. Changes may therefore be covertly and effectively resisted.

THE LOGIC AND DETAIL VERSUS THE VISIONARY SWEEP

In view of the scientific and engineering backgrounds that most R&D people have, a concern with detail and logic is very common. Technologists are trained in quantitative techniques of mathematics and statistics and, probably, modelling. They are accustomed to abstracting the essentials of any situation and addressing them in a disciplined way.

Even a firmwide change program has to be clearly argued and justified. R&D people want to understand not only the why but the when and the how of any changes that are going to have an impact on the firm, and on their part of the organization, in particular. The message that the firm will be expecting growth and an increase in shareholder value from better management of its technology base is difficult enough to get across. The concept of moving from a totally introverted organization, where all R&D is undertaken internally, to one which is more open, better able to communicate with the rest of the firm, able to network with external experts, and perhaps move toward a virtual R&D organization is one that will meet some fierce resistance. There is some truth in the perception that R&D organizations, highly science- and engineering-driven, have a limited appreciation of the business issues driving the need for change of this magnitude.

THE FIRM MUST FIND WAYS OF CROSSING THE CULTURAL DIVIDE

If the chief executive and senior members of the management team want to improve the efficiency and effectiveness of the R&D organization, they must recognize, early on, what could face them and decide how they are going to address the R&D cultural issues. At one extreme, they can make sure that the change program is undertaken logically, with lots of consensus with the R&D organization, lots of team building, using external consultants as facilitators, and spending significant time and money to turn the organization around. Alternatively, they may decide to adopt a type of control culture and make rapid changes without necessarily going through a very long and protracted change program, as some European R&D organizations and many Japanese firms do. Here, the innovation process tends to take place within an environment that lays down strict organizational rules, procedures, and hierarchies, and where failure, particularly at the individual level, can often result in some form of corporate punishment.

The decision is one that only the chief executive and senior management can make. It is influenced, however, by the current state of the business, the current potential for the R&D organization to meet the short- and longer-term aspirations of the business, and the patience of the shareholders. Whichever their preference, however, better communication is going to be critical if misunderstandings are to be avoided and sensitivities are to be acknowledged. If there is time for the consensus approach, cultural barriers can be very effectively broken down by a process of staff rotation, both within the local organization and abroad. The process of staff rotation, however, is probably easier from the R&D organization into the rest of the business rather than vice versa.

IMPROVED COMMUNICATION

One of the keys to success in managing change and overcoming cultural barriers within the firm is improved communications. Misunderstanding and conflict often occur as a result of poor communication. It is imperative that other business units understand how to communicate effectively with their R&D colleagues, bearing in mind their need for logic, clarity, and detail.

In an international environment, the potential problems may be compounded. If the marketing department, for example, is relying on its international R&D network to come up with creative product development opportunities, it must understand not only the basic R&D language but also must take into account the different responses that are likely to derive from different national cultures. A U.S. technology center or laboratory, for example, may promote values of high individualism, risk taking, equalization of rank and position, and a culture that looks on a failure (provided it doesn't happen too regularly) as being part of the learning process. Alternatively, in Japan, there are strict organizational rules, procedures, and hierarchy where failure is often punished. In the United Kingdom, punishment of the guilty for creative ideas that do not deliver on the original objectives means that risk taking is to be avoided. The marketing department and business unit managers must therefore be aware of these differences and allocate projects accordingly.

JOB ROTATION

Where a protective screen has been allowed to develop around the R&D organization, it gets harder and harder to shift. One way of breaking down this barrier is to organize systematic job rotations through different parts of the organization. Ideally, those involved should be the high flyers within the R&D organization who are going to be able to influence and change the culture in line with the overall objectives of the firm. Training seminars, both nationally and internationally, can help create a shared culture and also develop a network of contacts throughout the firm to help build an informal but effective communication process.

International Experience

International assignments are an excellent way of breaking down cultural barriers and transferring best practice between parts of the organization. If transfers on long-term assignments are not possible, another option is to set up individual project teams with multibusiness-unit and multinational participants.

Managers get a better perspective on how people can be encouraged to work together and communicate better if they visit foreign R&D centers and attend regular senior management meetings at which key projects are reviewed, achievements are updated, and the corporate business and technology strategies are continually reinforced.

This process, however, is both complex and very costly. The involvement of the HR department is critical in ensuring that the most effective results are obtained from any such program of interchange, transfer, and multinational project involvement.

SOME ORGANIZATIONAL REORIENTATION MAY BE REQUIRED TO SUPPORT BUSINESS CHANGES

Senior managers in multinational organizations cannot fail to have been touched by the word "globalization." The global enterprise is being driven by developments in information technology, which make access to data on markets and customers around the world virtually instantaneous. Firms in the financial sector, which track movements in the prices of stocks and shares from Tokyo through London and on to New York as the earth rotates and dawn breaks on each continent, are the most obvious example.

Many firms assert that they think and act globally, and many of them have undertaken a fundamental restructuring of their business processes, their supporting IT systems, and their organizational structures to facilitate the move to globalization. Yet, the R&D organization has, by and large, escaped. It has become adept at protecting its own identity rather than aligning itself with the needs of the business. It can no longer be allowed to escape attention. Some organizational change is going to be required in R&D to support the global evolution of the business. That organizational change will not, however, be based on the old debate about centralization versus decentralization, nor will it simply be a question of moving the boxes on the organization chart. Forceful leadership from the very top must sweep away the argument over a centralized or decentralized entity, and old hierarchical constraints must give way to business needs.

STRONG LEADERSHIP WILL BRING R&D INTO THE HEART OF THE BUSINESS, REGARDLESS OF ITS LOCATION

Most R&D organizations were originally established at or near the primary location of the company. As the number of personnel grew, they were often relocated to their own specialized laboratories or technical centers deep in the countryside. This was the typical setup for the very large and centralized R&D organizations of major firms in the 1960s and 1970s.

The 1980s saw the introduction of the concept of decentralized R&D. This was based on having a corporate R&D group which set long-term project priorities. Within individual business units, short- and medium-term projects were assigned to laboratories and technical centers that were distributed nationally or, in the case of the evolving multinational organization, across many countries. The trend in the 1990s and into the next millennium will be the development of the outsourced or virtual R&D organization. This concept builds on the decentralized structures introduced in the 1980s.

The debate about centralized versus decentralized R&D, however, continues to rage or to bubble to the surface regularly. As funding of R&D receives more and more attention, less money may be made available for research, and the central R&D organization will have a smaller role to play. The reallocation of development activities to R&D functions in operating units across the world means that they will come under more pressure to deliver product responses to meet local market demands. Remnants of corporate R&D may survive to provide overall strategic direction, to set up collaborative R&D projects (using internal and external sources), and so on. The key to success is not, however, how R&D is managed, but whether it demonstrates real leadership in what it does to deliver effective and sustainable growth to the business.

THE CHIEF EXECUTIVE CANNOT ABROGATE ULTIMATE RESPONSIBILITY FOR R&D

The chief executive is expected to be something of a god—getting involved in all the key functions of the firm and all its key projects. This is, of course, impossible, but the chief executive of a technology-based firm *does* have to get involved with the technology. Although possibly intimidated by the technologists and the new technology that the firm is operating, the CEO must not duck the need to be involved in the technological decisions of the firm. Given the rate of technological change and the introduction of multifunctional technologies, CEOs have a unique role to play in ensuring that business and technology strategies are fused effectively and efficiently.

He or she does not have to be a scientist, a technologist, or an engineer, although recent surveys in the United Kingdom and the United States indicate that companies led by technical or marketing people, in general, substantially outperform those run by financial managers. In a technology-based firm, however, the executive needs to understand about technology management in his or her industry. This understanding is acquired by asking the right questions, couched in the right language, the business language of the firm.

THE CHIEF TECHNOLOGY OFFICER SERVES AS THE CEO's ADVISER AND CONFIDANT

CEOs therefore probably need excellent chief technology officers (CTOs), who should act as their conscience. The chief technology officer does not automatically become the confidant and right arm of the chief executive. She or he must first show an understanding of the broader issues facing the business and should be able to relate to the concerns of the chief executive and to provide the questions that should be asked of all the technologists within the firm. In other words, the CTO helps the chief executive develop technology communication and language skills.

The chief technology officer is not necessarily the best technologist in the firm, although many have been promoted through the organization primarily for their scientific or technology skills. More important are business and managerial skills, the ability to translate the chief executive's vision for the firm into technical reality and to be rigorous in assessing the technological direction of the firm and developments in the market and the industry. CTOs must also be capable of managing a dynamic portfolio of technology development and innovation projects and delivering real shareholder value from that portfolio of projects. They must understand where and how to acquire the best technologies throughout the world and to apply them in the most effective and efficient manner within a virtual R&D organization.

The CTO should not be interested in the size of the R&D budget, the number of staff he or she controls, or personal standing within the scientific or technical community. On the other hand, the core competencies within her or his organization should be a prime concern, where particular capability or competencies are missing, and how to fill these, either by recruiting or by developing partnerships and alliances with other organizations. With the senior R&D management team, the CTO will be able to allocate resources to those projects that are really going to deliver value for the shareholders.

When chief technology officers are doing the job well, they are seen to be key influencers in decisions made by the chief executive relating to the overall direction of the firm. They are not regarded as the head of "fortress R&D" but as respected members of senior management—probably serving on the board—and able to facilitate and enhance the interfaces to other organizational units within the firm.

A CTO's role in supporting the chief executive is critical to the success of the firm. With the right relationship, these two people can drive significant growth in revenue and profit for the firm. Together, they can manage, direct, and lead a change process that is driven by a rapidly changing technological environment. The reward for the chief technology officer who gets it right is a good shot at becoming the next chief executive.

BUSINESS NEEDS MUST TAKE PRECEDENCE OVER HIERARCHICAL CONSTRAINTS

The chief technology officer also must recognize that the hierarchy within R&D is irrelevant and that line management should be an enabler of delivering projects, not a constraint. The more advanced organizations are moving to a process where project-specific teams, often with their own project budgets, are set up and broken down according to the life of the project. As a result, roles are changed from project to project. Project leaders are assigned according to their strengths and previous experience in similar roles. Project leaders who show that they can operate in short, sharp bursts, under pressure, will lead rapid development projects; those who are good at leading long-run, complex, high-risk projects will also have their strengths exploited by the firm.

The flexible and learning organization is one that recognizes that by playing to the managerial and communications strengths of its people (taking, as given, their strengths in biology, physics, mechanical engineering, and so on), it creates for those people much more fulfilling and enjoyable roles in the organization. It also enables the firm to develop dynamic processes across the whole of R&D, based on expertise both within the firm and from external resources.

***

There is no doubt that creating the right culture and organizational processes can have a major impact on the way R&D performs. By focusing on processes and outputs and linking the outputs to the needs of the market, R&D can be a major contributor to revenue and profit growth, rather than a cost. Once these elements are in place, the firm can really address the goal of implementing global R&D and innovation processes to enable it to be a world leader.

CASE STUDY—CENTRO RICERCHE FIAT

R&D is not about selling research but competitiveness.

GIAN CARLO MICHELLONE

President and Chief Executive, Centro Ricerche Fiat

In June 1994 an article in *Business Week* magazine reviewed spending on R&D by leading companies across Europe, the U.S., and Asia. In the survey Fiat S.p.A. was shown as one of the world's most improved companies in terms of increased R&D efficiency, particularly because Fiat's R&D organization, Centro Ricerche Fiat (CRF), had managed to optimize available funding by ditching marginal projects, decentralizing R&D efforts, creating project teams to own product ideas from the laboratory to the market, and working out ways to collaborate fruitfully with outside experts from other companies, consortiums, and universities.

The largest private research center in Italy, CRF was founded in 1976 as one of the 15 sectors of the Fiat Group. Currently employing over 850 researchers with an annual turnover of $75 million, CRF's main mission is to transfer to operating centers innovative products, processes, and methodologies in five main areas of technological specialization: engines, vehicles, electronic systems, processes and materials, and optomechanical technologies.

CRF President and Chief Executive, Gian Carlo Michellone, believes that a key factor for keeping in touch with the market is to focus attention, right from the beginning of research, not only on the technology but also on the customer, whom he defines as being in two distinct categories:

Macrocustomers are the managers responsible for seeing that a particular innovation is developed. They are involved in making decisions concerning the financing of research projects and subsequent investment and modifications within the organization to receive ideas from CRF and then to transfer that technology into the marketplace.

Microcustomers are managers who implement innovations developed and transferred by CRF. Microcustomers often have to reevaluate their own knowledge, status, and behavior because CRF's recommendations may be substantial, and the receiving unit in the customer sometimes demonstrates a tendency to oppose change owing to the "not invented here" syndrome.

Thus it is the macrocustomers who give the order for research to take place, whereas microcustomers assist them to implement the results of the research. Michellone considers both to be of great importance to the continuing success of CRF, and this is why he places so much emphasis on defining who his customers are.

Gian Carlo Michellone first became involved in the Fiat Group's R&D program in the 1970s when he assessed antibrake technology from U.S. companies for potential import into the company. Based on his review, Fiat decided to commit to Michellone the development of the technology which Fiat sold as patents in the United States. Placed in charge of engineering systems for IVECO, Michellone was made Managing Director of a new joint venture with Rockwell International Corporation. In 1985 he joined the newly formed innovation division of Fiat Auto and by 1987 had taken on responsibility for the development of all Fiat Auto products. With the setting up of the new organization of Fiat Auto in 1989, Michellone transferred to CRF as its President and Chief Executive.

In 1993 CRF faced a major crisis when Fiat's business units reduced their funding levels by 30 percent, an event which followed four years of budget growth and an increase in head count. Reacting to the shortfall, Michellone decided that CRF needed much more of a market orientation and that fresh external funding was urgently required, particularly from the European Union and small to medium sized companies. In addition, Michellone says, "I decided that a fundamental change was required in the makeup of staff in order to change the culture of the organization."

As a result of his actions, two key outputs were achieved. First, from the position in 1993 where virtually all of CRF's funding came from the Fiat Group, today only 70 percent of revenues come from research undertaken for the parent company. The rest comes from the European Union and other customers. Indeed, CRF is now one of the biggest receivers of European funding into R&D programs where the emphasis is on development rather than pure research. Second, in the past five years total turnover of CRF staff has been about 60 percent, a deliberate policy which is expected to continue. "The average age of research staff in CRF is 36," says Michellone, "which guarantees a continuous flow of innovative ideas."

In addition, CRF is now fully responsible for its own budget. It must sell its services to the rest of the Fiat Group, and where there is a shortfall in R&D capacity against what is sold to Fiat, it is allowed to provide services even to competitors. For example, CRF has recently done business with Mercedes, Detroit Diesel, and Renault on various studies and developments for new engines.

Again, following on from the 1993 crisis, Michellone has focused on R&D opportunities in the European market rather than concentrating solely on Fiat or indeed in Italy alone. Because R&D was regarded within the Fiat Group as a cost center, Michellone has fought to change this perception to one where others would share his basic philosophy that the R&D of the group must focus on the sector in which it specializes and, in particular, on its key markets and customers. He believes passionately that an R&D organization can only survive in the long run by meeting its customers' needs. In his words, "R&D is not about selling research, but competitiveness."

This focus on customers is encapsulated in CRF's mission phrase, "competitiveness for customers at competitive prices." CRF's "obsession" with customers is highlighted particularly by the ability of the organization to deliver positive outputs and results to customers from CRF's development programs. This focus on customers means that each year CRF is able to undertake various measures including assessment of micro-customers in terms of their percentage R&D expenditure, the overall R&D budget for CRF by customer, the impact of projects proposed by the innovation committee, and how CRF is going to develop its forward innovation plans.

The outputs from this work result in three categories of R&D program:

- Projects where CRF and the customer are innovation followers
- Projects where CRF and the customer are providing products which are not yet on the market
- "Son of a bitch" or innovative developments where there are probably as many opportunities for major failure as there are for achieving major winners

Where competitors are concerned, Michellone has a refreshing attitude. "In some instances it is clear that a clash is inevitable, particularly with competing projects applying for European Union funding. But I also see that CRF has a vital role to play in setting up joint ventures and alliances with competitors in order to maximize the knowledge and expertise of the organization and others who can complement our development skills."

Patent protection is a good example of CRF's, and Michellone's, attitude toward competitors. Basically, the philosophy of CRF is not to drive hard to retain IPR or patents. For example, a high pressure diesel ignition system was recently sold to Bosch, including the know-how. The reason for this is that Michellone believes most organizations can quite easily maneuver around patent protection, so he considers it pointless to spend time and money defending them. The key issue for him is to develop a continuous process for refreshing and renewing the product line.

In this respect, future products that CRF is working on include the development of methane fuelled cars, optics and electronic systems for new types of lamps, the application of lasers within the car, and self-drive cars. In addition, CRF is looking to provide the development resources and undertake development projects for firms outside the automotive sector.

In looking back over the years it is clear that Fiat management allowed CRF a great deal of time and freedom to change from a traditional R&D organization to one which is much more dynamic and innovative today. According to Michellone, "The catalyst for the change was that R&D was regarded as too expensive and the business units cut back the amount of money that they would invest in what was regarded as a cost overhead."

The change to a more dynamic and entrepreneurial organization has benefited both CRF and Fiat as a company. The total focus on customers and the method of funding development projects, not only from Fiat but other organizations, has transformed it into one of the most dynamic R&D centers in Europe.

THE CHIEF EXECUTIVE'S GUIDE

Many of the points covered in this book can be turned into a relatively simple checklist of questions that a chief executive can ask of the scientists and technologists in the firm.

1. WHY?

Why do we have an R&D group in the firm?

Given that we have an R&D group and it is the keeper of our technology strategy:

- How is the technology strategy integrated and linked to our business strategy?
- What is our technology strategy for the coming five years?
- What is the quality of the technology strategy, and is it implementable?

Does the technology strategy clearly define the R&D portfolio in terms of customer service developments, projects which are derivatives of the existing product portfolio, next-generation projects, and product breakout projects?

In terms of the portfolio:

- Does it match the technology strategy?
- Does it have the right balance of projects with the right mix in terms of risk, time of delivery?
- How is the portfolio generated and updated?

Which three R&D projects in our product portfolio are going to deliver the maximum financial return to the business over the next one to two years? What impact is this increased business going to have on shareholder value?

2. WHAT?

What are we doing in R&D and how do we decide what to do?
In particular:

- What are the financial and market criteria that justify our top R&D projects?
- What measures of R&D performance are used for projects and individual R&D units, and what do they show?
- What is the R&D budget and how is it managed?
- What is the quality of the output from the R&D organization?

In terms of the how:

- How are projects generated, justified, and approved?
- How are projects stopped? How many have we stopped over the last two years, and how well does the process work?
- How is our technology base categorized in terms of existing projects (enabling, critical, pacing)?
- How big is the R&D organization, and how does this compare with those of our competitors?
- How does our technology compare to our competitor's?

3. WHEN?

When are results delivered to our customers?
  In terms of time to market:

- How is it managed?
- What performance have we achieved over the last two to five years?
- Are too many projects being attempted concurrently?
- What is the history of delivery of results?

  In terms of flexibility to adapt programs:

- How easy is it to change the R&D program?
- What happens when the market changes during one of our major development programs?
- Do we have too many small projects which are clogging up and delaying the delivery of our key projects?

4. WHO?

In terms of the organization:

- What are the numbers and mix of skills in relation to the tasks that have to be undertaken?
- What organizational structure are we using and does it work?
- What is the quality of our R&D team(s)?

  In terms of the capabilities and competencies:

- What are our key capabilities and competencies?
- What are our behavioral and cultural competencies?
- What is the morale, energy, and sense of purpose of the group?

- What management style is used within the organization?
- How innovative are our people?

5. HOW?

How is work actually performed?

- What is the quality of project management?
- What is the quality and discipline of project reporting?
- How are resources allocated to tasks?
- Do we have the right infrastructure?
- Is the appropriate IT support in place?
- How do communications happen between R&D and the rest of the firm, suppliers, and customers?

In terms of R&D processes:

- Are they documented?
- Do they represent best practice (for example, concurrent engineering)?
- Are the documented methods adhered to?

6. WHERE?

Where is the R&D work performed?

- Are the numbers and locations of R&D facilities appropriate to current needs?
- Do we have an appropriate mix between internal and external resourcing (virtual R&D)?
- Why do we have to perform any of the R&D functions internally?

* * *

If chief executives are interested in improving the performance of their R&D organizations, they should be able to get answers to all of the previous questions within an eight-week period. They must not allow the technologists to bog them down in trivia, detail, too much technical mumbo jumbo, or excuses as to why this information cannot be obtained. The mere fact of asking such questions in the organization will send shock waves through the system, but this is only the beginning of the task. Thereafter, chief executives have to manage a change program for R&D within their firms to deliver growth.

INDEX

ABOUT THE AUTHOR

John Buckley, Group Head of the Global Technology division of PA Consulting Group, one of the world's leading management and technology consulting firms, specializes in helping clients manage technology to deliver growth and increase shareholder value. Mr. Buckley's division has worked with many international companies, including Shell, Phillips, Pfizer, and GlaxoWellcome.

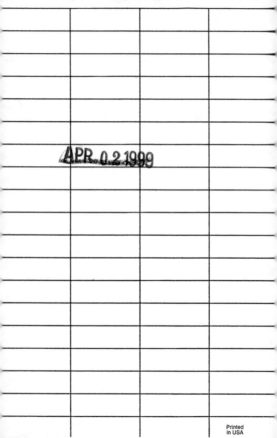

DATE DUE

APR 0 2 1999

Printed in USA